From Hill to Sea:

Dispatches from the Fife Psychogeographical

Collective 2010 - 2014

By

The Fife Psychogeographical Collective

From Hill to Sea: Dispatches from the Fife
Psychogeographical Collective 2010 – 2014

By The Fife Psychogeographical Collective

Publisher: Bread and Circuses 2015
www.breadandcircusespublishing.com

ISBN   9781625178879

Cover design by Vincent Pacheco
www.VincentPacheco.com

Book layout/Design by Martin J. Coffee
Coffee2go Editing Solutions
martin.coffee@gmail.com
http://coffee2go.weebly.com/

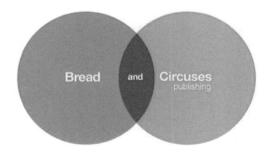

It is not down in any map; true places never are.

Herman Melville

A schizophrenic out for a walk is a better model than a neurotic lying on the analyst's couch. A breath of fresh air, a relationship with the outside world.

Gilles Deleuze and Félix Guattari, *Anti-Oedipus.*

'It's comin' yet for a' that'

This book selects, collects and remixes selected dispatches from the Fife Psychogeographical Collective ("FPC") archive over the period 2010 – 2014.

We firmly believe that walking can be a liberating and radical act wherever you may find yourself.

^ ^ ^

Field trips, general wanderings and rag-pickings from hill to sea

Mapping the interstices of past, present and possible

From the Kingdom of Fife and beyond

≈ ≈ ≈

Contents

Why Fife?

A virtual island interzone, betwixt and between the cities of Edinburgh and Dundee; an ancient Pictish Kingdom, bounded by the Firths of Forth and Tay. Where a New Town is built on a 4,000 year old henge and 18 feet menhirs brood on a ladies golf course, under the shadow of Largo Law. Not far away, the statue of Alexander Selkirk, gazes out, projecting his own haunting presence into the psychogeographic mindscape. If Selkirk was the inspiration for Defoe's *Robinson Crusoe*, it is the ghost of Robinson who wanders and stalks through many a tract of the psychogeographic imagination. Witness Rimbaud's supposedly derived verb *robinsonner* (to travel mentally, or let the mind wander) or the unseen and unheard researcher in Patrick Keiller's films *London, Robinson in Space and Robinson in Ruins*.

Ideas crackle, tussle and fizz, throughout the ether over this Scottie dog's heid:

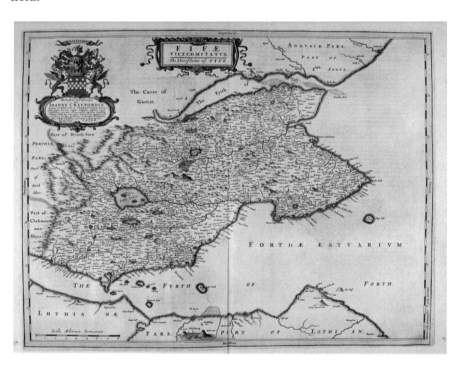

Kirkcaldy's famous son Adam Smith tossed a large brick into the pool of economic theory with a *The Wealth of Nations* (and let us not forget *The Theory of Moral Sentiments*) written on a site now housing Greggs the Bakers. The self-interest of the baker to supply us with Steak Bakes is alive and well. (The debate as to whether Smith, the moral philosopher, has been hijacked by the right will be left for another day). There is also a hauntology of radical socialism. In Cowdenbeath, Lawrence Storione founded the Anarchist Communist League and West Fife elected Willie Gallacher as the first Communist MP. In Lumphinnans you will find Gagarin Way, a street tagged in honour of the Soviet cosmonaut and from which Gregory Burke named his first play.

Concrete hippos and dinosaurs traverse the urban landscape in Glenrothes; cup and ring marks lie mute on The Binn (Hill) at Burntisland whilst a green witch's shop sits on the high street of Aberdour to deliver up soothing potions to the contemporary unwell. A secret bunker channels cold war paranoia and the devil is reputedly buried on Kirkcaldy beach, interred by the occult energies of the dark magus Michael Scot.

These are just a few random scatterings from this space of possibilities. 'A beggar's mantle fringed with gold'... a palimpsest of histories and vibrations. A site for exploration.

4th August 2010

Field Trips: Zones, Roads & Paths (with assorted Rag-Pickings)

Into the Void

It is often the shortest journey, undertaken with least expectation, which offers up an excess of possibility beyond what we expect to see.

It is always worth exploring the other side of the barbed wire fence.

Never keep to the path.

(Extracts from FPC Field Guide).

Time constrained by commitments later on in the day and yet compelled by the *need* to go for a walk, we settle on a local part of the Fife Coastal Path. The very short stretch between Inverkeithing and Dalgety Bay is a narrow tarmacadam / cinder ribbon of a mile, or so, that meanders around the coastline. Whilst offering fine views of the Forth Rail Bridge and over to Edinburgh and Arthur's Seat it is unlikely to trouble any tourist brochure. Indeed, the walking guide for the Fife Coastal Path devotes one short paragraph to it. There is a clear implication that this is a space that you can simply pass through. It is also a functional path, popular with dog walkers, leisurely strollers and is even lined with street lighting. However, as the sign above indicates, the traveller is asked to keep within the marked path. We cannot help thinking of Little Red Riding Hood but can only read the sign as an invitation to stray...

There is a distinctive topography to the land along this stretch of the path which edges around Inverkeithing Bay with sloping scrub and wooded elevations up to Preston Hill and Letham Hill behind. These factors and lack of road access, has prevented any urban coalescence between the nodal points of the old industrial harbour of Inverkeithing and the 1960s new town of Dalgety Bay.

Looking towards Dalgety Bay from Inverkeithing

However, there is also a distinct feeling of crossing a threshold, as you escape the gravity and material ephemera of the human settlement, and move into this *zone* from either end. A feeling of the wildness encroaching, long forgotten histories written into the land, whispered stories at the periphery of perception. A freeing up of the rules.

~ ~ ~

Lock-ups - Leaving Inverkeithing

Leaving from Inverkeithing, we walk past a row of lock-ups, which are not without some semblance of aesthetic beauty in their irregular order and contrasting colours. You wonder what is behind these out-of-the-way closed doors? Some have obviously not been accessed for some time given the overgrown vegetation in front. We also notice that as soon as you pass the last lock-up, the wild space is already there, encroaching green fingers, edging into the human space and into the photo frame. There is also a rather cryptic graffiti announcement:

We are not sure whether to read this utterance as a comment on some existentialist predicament ("Out of it") or a marker post to signify a transition point of moving out of the urban setting. (Moving oot it). Later on, when we reach the Dalgety Bay end of the path we find more graffiti on the first inhabited house. There is a clear sense that both of these graffiti bookend an entry - or exit. We read these signs as an intimation that what lies between these threshold markers is a different place - *a zone*. Not urban, yet not rural. Not even 'classic' edgeland. Instead, an indication that what lies within is an escape from the ostensible order of the settlements. Possibly a play area, a hidden place, an out of sight place, a gathering place, a wildness.

We are not far out of Inverkeithing when our advice to keep to the marked path is quickly discounted. We are drawn to the barbed wire topped, chain wire fence that we can see across a flat area of post-industrial wasteland off to the left. It's a pretty feeble attempt at preventing access as a whole section has been removed and most of the barbed wire has been snipped off.

We follow the well-trodden desire path through the fence to find ourselves in the heart of the abandoned Prestonhill Quarry, now filled up with water. There is a compelling, uncanny beauty to this place. A void gouged and hewn out of the Earth, with the remaining dolerite walls reflecting weak sunlight like a cubist canvas. The acoustic ambience has also noticeably changed. We are in a huge reverberating chamber so that the slightest noise pings around the walls. A distant ice cream van sounds as if it should be coming from somewhere within the quarry, possibly submerged underneath the water. At the same time swallows dart and zig-zag above our heads, whilst magpies hop and skip around the top rocks, observing us with curiosity. A couple of buzzards circle in the distance. There is no one else around.

Prestonhill Quarry - Cubist Walls I

What is noticeable is that even in these most barren of conditions, non-human nature is re-staking a claim with outcrops of growing vegetation, clinging to the quarry walls, thriving in the most hostile of conditions and the thinnest scrapings of soil.

We soon find the ubiquitous discarded fridge. Lying face down, its broken body surrounded by other accumulated fly tipped debris. The human stain of the dumping ground. It is always a puzzle to consider the time and energy it must take to fly tip a fridge in an 'out of the way' area, such as this, compared with taking it to the recycling point. Perhaps it's for the sheer visceral thrill of throwing a fridge into a quarry. We assume that it has been pushed over the top and has been there for some time.

~~~

There is perhaps another attraction of the quarry. It is an unseen place with very deep water.   Every surface has another side. What else lurks underneath the skin of calm blue water? What is submerged down there in the green depths with the little fishes?

~~~~~

g

o

i

n

g

~~~~~

b

e

l

o

w

~~~~~

t

h

e

~~~~~

s

u

r

f

a

c

e

~~~~~~~~~~~~~~~

It would appear that the quarry is also a favoured disposal spot for stolen cars, making for an ideal symbiotic relationship with the diving community who find the quarry an attractive destination for underwater exploration. There is plenty to see and investigate below the surface. We are also told later that local fishermen stock the quarry with fish which they then try to catch again, fostering a fledgling underwater eco-system. The rumours that someone may have introduced a pike are confirmed by this evidence:

All underwater photographs of the quarry are © 'Lindsay Brown aka Stray Seal. Used with permission and thanks.

~ ~ ~

The quarry is also clearly a gathering place. A hidden place of escape and unregulated recreation. We walk around the void, recording some of the many tags that have been written on to the rocks.

Staring up at the quarry wall and contemplating the material passage of time ossified in these rocks. The play of light on the angular shapes conjures up dynamic planes of movement and appear to imbue the rocks with an almost animistic quality. We can eventually see a cubist rock giant, emerging from time with right arm raised:

Emerging Cubist Rock Giant

~~~

Back on the path, we head off to the right hand side this time.

Stretching out over the water is a fretwork pier of rusting metal which we find out later was the old industrial conveyor system used to load the quarried stone on to tethered ships.

We stand for a while to listen out for the lost sounds of this place. The kling klang ghosts of the industrial machinery, the heft of monolithic slabs of dolerite rattling down towards the waiting ships.

almost silent now

now almost silent

only the ack-ack-ack

of a solitary gull

riding the wind currents

overhead.

A large steel plate has been placed across the structure presumably in an attempt to prevent people from climbing out along the pier. It's unlikely to be a deterrent but it no doubt satisfies some health and safety regime. The plate has rusted and weathered into something resembling a Richard Serra sculpture:

Richard Serra Was Here?

Once again, we can see how the wildness is staking its claim with tendrils of green growing up, through and out of the lattice structure. "Shugg and Leanne" evidence of the human urge to make a mark. The basic proof of existence. A name recorded. A demonstration of love?

Running parallel to the fretwork structure is another abandoned jetty. The pulleys remain suspended from the cross beam conjuring up something of the gibbet or perhaps some form of cosmic launch mechanism to project the traveller up and into the pillows of cloud:

all of this

abandoned history

lost stories, forgotten stories

sounds of absence

whispering in the wind.

We decide to explore a bit further underneath the conveyor structure sensing that this may yield possibilities. We are not disappointed when we alight on this gathering site:

What is noticeable is that there is no rubbish strewn here. It's as if this is a place of respect. Strangely enough, the atmosphere evokes a similar feel to another outcrop of rocks that can be found on The Binn (Hill) along the coast at Burntisland:

Rock outcrop, The Binn, Burntisland

Humans have also made their marks on The Binn stones, albeit some 4,000 years earlier

Cup and Ring, The Binn, Burntisland

~ ~ ~

We pick up a bit of walking pace to take advantage of the seascape:

a sounded wave, persistent and seductive -

plays the shoreline.

flux and flow of sea brine -

a spilling over

of elemental energy.

Once again the unusual topography is such that we can hear a mash-up of field and hedgerow bird song against foreshore waders and gull talk. A chorus of crows, darting finches and tits; a wren bobs along the wall before taking refuge in the trees. What looks like a falling red leaf is actually a robin. On the foreshore, oystercatchers, and curlews wade and waddle whilst fulmars, cormorants and herring gulls dive and swoop. Symphonies of birdsong and gull chatter.

It doesn't take long to reach Dalgety Bay, but just before the threshold graffiti we come across this:

Abandoned House Dalgety Bay

Roofless and abandoned, it looks as if all of the surrounding land has been sucked away from the foundations leaving it sitting like an old tooth stump.

We try to piece together a narrative here but fail. Why has it been abandoned? Why left to ruin? It was clearly a property that had wealth behind it at some point, sitting in its walled garden. Enquiries are made of a few passing locals but yield nothing. "It's always been like that" says a man who looks to be in his forties. "Ever since I was a wee kid". He doesn't know the story though.

~~~

We are on the reverse trip back to Inverkeithing when we spot a small opening in the stone wall with a signpost:

How could we resist? Off up the rickety path which didn't appear overly well trodden.

We find a beetle on its back on one of the steps clearly distressed. A multitude of legs. Flailing wildly, unable to right itself. We soon tip it on to its feet and the little jet black shell scuffles off into the grass.

The path ascends fairly steeply and it's not long before we find ourselves on a high ridge which slopes away towards Letham Wood. That will have to wait for another day. Our immediate area of interest lies off to the left. Another barbed wire fence and it's as easy to circumvent as the last one. This is what we had been leading up to. We could already feel what we were about to witness but were unprepared for the sheer scale of it. Compared to the ground level, water-filled heart of the quarry, we could now gain a perspective of the entire void and walk right up to peer over the edge.

The Void

Peering over the side, into the void, it's as if a vacuum is trying to suck your insides out. I'm reminded of Aragon in *Paris Peasant* and the 'suicide bridge' in Buttes Chaumont park - coincidentally built in a reclaimed stone quarry. Before metal grilles were erected along the side of the bridge, it would supposedly claim victims from passers-by who had had no intention whatsoever of killing themselves but found themselves suddenly tempted by the invocation of the abyss.

Our photographic skills are unable to adequately capture the scale of this almost mournful absence, hewn from the Earth. It's a place to simply sit and stare for a while.

.

.

.

.

.

It's often easy to forget to raise our heads to the horizon. Having escaped the seduction of the void, we now realise how high up on the ridge we are. It changes our sense of the whole topography of the area. We can see how connected we are to the East side of Inverkeithing and marvel at the long view over to Dunfermline. We can see <u>Spinner</u> in the distance with the distorted perspective making it appear as if it is growing out of a housing estate.

Spinner

We later discover that there is also an abandoned WW2 radio station complete with intact pill boxes not too far away but don't see them today. Another time.

We descend back down the hill to the coastal path and reflect on our experience. What we had anticipated as a short, local coastal walk had been transformed into something else. A journey through a zonal space teeming with encounters and traces of the human, non-human and even the animistic. A co-existence of dumping ground, liminal playground, gathering place and nature sanctuary. The transient narrative of human activity inscribed in the abandoned house and the mute quarries and jetties a reminder of how financial capital abandons one exhausted void to migrate to the next site of profitable extraction.

Above all of this, the continually changing drama in the sky:

Sometimes it's in the sky when you look - Buzzard dots

Eye in the Sky

And as we return to Inverkeithing we can smell the sweet wood lying in the still functioning timber yard and take one last photo. It's only later, that we notice that in this photograph, and almost all of the others, there is some intimation of wild nature straying into the frame.

An alert wildness, observing, perhaps patiently waiting for its moment to come.

~~~~~~

This has been a little slice of:

From The

Now Playing: James Plotkin: Mark Spybey - *A Peripheral Blur*

24th October 2012

Now playing: Mothlite - 'The One in the Water' from *Flax of Reverie*

8th November 2014 (Revised to incorporate Stray Seal photographs)

a

thinking   space

for

place   thinking

No Noise at the Pithead

Industrial ghost - winding gear of the Frances Pit Dysart.

8th February 2014

Now playing: Matt Berry - *Kill the Wolf*

Crows, Crowns and a Curious Landscape

Like animated clods of black earth suspended in the branches. A murder of crows.

We can feel their collective beady gaze following us as we walk down the single-track road that leads into the hamlet of Pattiesmuir. A fluttering of wings and more descend. It is hard not to think of the gathering flocks in Hitchcock's *The Birds*.

For no apparent reason, they suddenly take flight. A spiralling vortex of wing, beak and claw, ascending, then wind-blown towards the white crosses in Douglas Bank Cemetery. Only four return to the upper branches, no longer interested in us. One looks west whilst three gaze towards the east indicating our direction of travel.

Three craws ...

The old car at the entrance to Pattiesmuir evokes a sense of time travel as we walk through an agricultural hamlet whose physical fabric has changed very little over the past 150 years. A collection of low-level whitewashed cottages line a single street that provides both entrance and exit with no through road.

Pattiesmuir has been recorded on maps as Patiemuir, Peattie Muir, Pettymuir and a number of other variants. An early map from 1654 records it as Pettimuir, although the origin of the name remains obscure. Local folklore suggests that the area was once a focus of Romany activity and even that The King of the Gypsies once had a 'palace' nearby. The 1896 Ordnance Survey map does refer to an area of trees to the west of the settlement as "Egyptian Clump", and a neighbouring field is also noted as "Egypt Field".

In the early 18th Century a small community of hand-loom weavers formed in Pattiesmuir to help supply the Dunfermline linen industry. By 1841 there was a population of 130 which supported a school - attended by 34 pupils - an Inn, a blacksmith and three public wells. By 1857 the population was 190. However, the introduction of the power-loom meant a slow decline in the fortunes of hand-loom weavers and by 1870 almost all weaving activity had ceased.

There are no schools or Inns in Pattiesmuir these days but a building called The College remains. Its origins lie in a fraternity of radical weavers who set up the 'college' so that weavers and agricultural workers could meet for self-improvement classes in politics, philosophy, economics and theology. They subscribed to the *Edinburgh Political and Literary Journal* and pooled funds to buy the works of Burns and the new Waverley novels of Walter Scott. One notable member and self-proclaimed 'professor' of the College was Andrew Carnegie, grandfather to a Dunfermline born grandson of the same name. Young 'Andra' would travel to America in 1848 and eventually consolidate the US steel industry to become the 'richest man in the world'.

You cannot drive through Pattiesmuir, but if you walk you can take a left where the road stops and walk into a curious area of landscape. Neither edgeland nor particularly rural it is bounded by Dunfermline, only a few miles away, to the north and Rosyth to the East. A rarely walked mix of hedgerows, old woodland, farm tracks and tenanted agricultural land. On Google maps it is an area that is deemed 'featureless'. However, we already know that it hosts a coffin road and the wild wood. Today's walk will reveal a few more surprises ...

We stand and watch the weather arrive. A huge palm of grey sky that threatens to smother us with rain but growls quickly past. Underfoot, attention is diverted to the heroic efforts of a slug traversing the rough stone path. The intensity of existence revealed in this waltzing fuselage of seal-smooth skin and striated hand-painted detail. Eventually it reaches more hospitable looking terrain and we can walk on.

We are intrigued by the sign on a set of ruined agricultural buildings. Clearly, it has been a long time since they were operational. Part of the roof is missing and internal vegetation is now stretching for the sun.

Minimal Disease Pigs - it could either be the name of an undiscovered hardcore punk band or a fragment from a Mark E. Smith lyric:

Beware of Guard - uh

Minimal Disease Pigs

No Entry

No Entry - uh

Of course, after the walk we had to find out what minimal disease pigs were:

Many infectious diseases are transferred from the sow to her offspring after birth and breaking this cycle of transference is the basis of the minimal disease concept. If piglets are reared in total isolation from their mother and all other pigs that are not minimal disease pigs (that is they never come in contact with or even breathe the same air as other pigs), they will not become infected with certain disease-causing organisms (pathogens) that are normally present in pigs. Thus the cycle of transfer of many organisms from one generation (the sow) to the next (her offspring) is broken.

There is an almost chilling bio-technocratic language behind this concept. A section on 'Breaking the Cycle' becomes even more so with descriptions of 'snatch farrowing', 'hysterectomy procurement techniques', 'euthanased sows' and 'total isolation rearing'. It would appear that the minimal disease nomenclature died out, in the UK, in the 1970s to be replaced by 'High Health Status'.

It is unclear what happened to the fortunes of this particular pig farm that is now being slowly reclaimed back into the landscape. An agricultural ruin that has given us a partial glimpse into the bio-technic world of the animal husbandry practices that deliver up packets of bacon and pork on to the supermarket shelves. Another connection that illustrates that the urban and rural, local and global can  never be viewed in isolation when we consider such basic questions as to how and where do we get our food.

As we head northwards towards the distant spires of Dunfermline, we encounter another relic of the agricultural past.

Crowned by thorns

an elegy

from the future?

An old petrol pump, presumably used at one time for filling up farm vehicles. Crowned by thorns, nature's brittle fingers have enveloped the head and spiralled down the structure. Any message that was once conveyed by the sign on the wall is completely effaced. At one level the image perhaps conveys a narrative of decline of the tenant farmer or small farmer in general. As food production becomes increasingly industrialised, the small farmer finds it uneconomic to compete. Like the pig-farm, the infrastructure is slowly being reclaimed by the natural world.

However, is there another narrative? The petrol pump as a potent symbol of the global petrochemical and energy industries that exploit non-renewable resources that will one day inevitably run out. What will the cost be to planet Earth and its lifeforms? Is a crown of thorns awaiting the petrochemical plants, power stations, cars, aeroplanes ...?

All questions to ponder as we head over the fields, nodding to the strange, silent wind poetry of Spinner. Just another story layered upon this 'featureless' curious landscape.

≈ ≈ ≈

Now playing: Hacker Farm – *UHF*

29th November 2014

References:

Department of Agriculture, Fisheries and Forestry, Queensland Government, Minimal Disease Pigs

Fife Council Enterprise Planning and Protective Services *Pattiesmuir Conservation Area Appraisal and Conservation Area Management Plan*, October 2011.

Raymond Lamont-Brown, *Carnegie: The Richest Man in the World* (Stroud: The History Press, 2006).

Some Questions of the Drift

i

"*I ask you:*

- What is the weight of light?"

- Clarice Lispector

ii

- What are the colours of time?

iii

- What are the sounds of the stones?

- When does the inside become the outside?

iv

v

- What is the material of memory?

- What would the trees think?

vi

vii

- What is the geography of a butterfly?

viii

- What is the shape of flight?

- When does the local become - the universal?

ix

- Where does the sky begin?

x

- What is the taste of place?

xi

xii

- Where are the energy flows?

xiii

- What is the future of the past?

xiv

- Who watches the watcher?

xv

- Who controls this space?

- Who determines the boundary?

xvi

xvii

xviii

xix

- Where is the coldness of the sun?

- What is the gravity of the moon?

xx

xxi

- Where is the boundary of night?

xxii

- Where is the future of freedom?

xxiii

- What is the distance of love?

xxiv

≈ ≈ ≈

(i)   Kirk Wynd, Kirkcaldy
(ii)   Merchant's House, Kirkcaldy
(iii)   Merchants House, Kirkcaldy II
(iv)   Rosyth Church – East Gable Inner – from West
(v)   St. Cuthbert's Churchyard, Edinburgh
(vi)   Devilla Forest, Fife
(vii)   Limekilns, Fife
(viii)   Lochore Meadows, Fife
(ix)   Burntisland from the Binn
(x)   Digbeth, Birmingham
(xi)   Café now Open – Digbeth Birmingham
(xii)   River Flow: Custard Factory, Digbeth
(xiii)   Abandoned factory, Digbeth
(xiv)   Sauchiehall Street, Glasgow
(xv)   George Square, Glasgow
(xvi)   Hadrian's Wall
(xvii)   The Berlin Wall
(xviii) Limekilns, Danger, Keep Out
(xix)   Sauchiehall Street, Glasgow
(xx)   At Mogwai play Zidane, Broomielaw, Glasgow
(xxi)   Rosyth Station, Car Park

Opening quote from Clarice Lispector's *The Hour of the Star*.

The photos of the Berlin Wall are from an inter-railing trip in the late 1980s. It was a coincidence to rediscover them in an old shoebox on the day that it was announced Lou Reed had died. I can still vividly recall a lurid, orange BASF cassette being pressed into my hand in the school playground. "Listen to this!" It was a recording of *Rock n Roll Animal*. Things changed.

I can still remember a number of the cassettes that travelled in the rucksack on that inter-railing adventure. *Berlin* was certainly one of them.

Now playing: Lou Reed - *Berlin*. RIP LR.

30th October 2013

Moby Dick, Laurie Anderson and The King's Cellar, Limekilns

*The book is so modern, it's insane. Melville uses all these voices —
historian, naturalist, botanist, lawyer, dreamer, obsessive librarian. His
jump-cut style is truly contemporary.*

Laurie Anderson on *Moby Dick*

November 1999

The métro pulls in to Bobigny Pablo-Picasso in the North Eastern suburbs
of Paris. Walking out on to Boulevard Maurice Thorez and up Boulevard
Lénine, it is apparent that this is a world apart from the Haussmanised
elegance left behind around forty minutes ago. Breaking free of the tourist
flocks on the Champs-Élysées, I had descended into the subterranean belly
of Charles de Gaulle Etoile to meet the familiar smell of the chthonic
underworld and the squeals, clangs and clatters of the metallic worms
burrowing through the entrails of the city. Doors explode open at each
métro stop to displace and gorge on the huddles and tentacles of drifting
humans in transit.

```
i        t
n        i
t        s
r        n
a        a
n        r
s        t
i        n
t        i
```

Up and down, to and from, the everyday life possibilities occurring directly
overhead: Ternes > Courcelles > Monceau > Villiers > Rome > Place de
Clichy > Blanche > Pigalle > Anvers > Barbès–Rochechouart > La Chapelle
> Stalingrad >...

A change at Jaurès to pick up line 5 and soon it's an ascent, emerging blinking
into bright daylight and this different world. Here, the streets are named after
artists and communist revolutionaries and the buildings remind me of the
Scottish New Towns: stark, brutalist and functional. Consulting my notebook
from the time I can see a handwritten scrawl:

Glenrothes!

The town where I grew up appears to have relocated to the Paris suburbs.

Bobigny - Prefecture Building   Fife Council Headquarters – Glenrothes

I was in Bobigny for the Festival d'Automne and heading to the MC93 Cultural Centre to see Laurie Anderson performing her 'multi-media' theatrical work *Songs and Stories From Moby-Dick*. Not a wholly accurate title as the piece is more of a meditation on Melville and what *that* book means to her. It was a fabulous experience to witness. The familiar Anderson performance tropes of expansive and existential themes, constructed instruments, minimal gestures and laconic storytelling were all brought to the fore. It certainly convinced me that there was more to this book than Ahab and his crew chasing a big fish. (ok mammal).

Then I read [Moby Dick] again. And it was a complete revelation. Encyclopedic in scope, the book moved through ideas about history, philosophy, science, religion, and the natural world towards Melville's complex and dark conclusions about the meaning of life, fear, and obsession. Being a somewhat dark person myself, I fell in love with the idea that the mysterious thing you look for your whole life will eventually eat you alive... [1]

For Anderson, Americans of her century and Melville's share certain unmistakable similarities: they are obsessive, technological, voluble and in search of the transcendental," she writes in the show's notes. It is this latter aspect — the meaning of life — which is the focus of "Songs and Stories," as Anderson asks Americans today, as Melville did in his lifetime: "What do you do when you no longer believe in the things that have driven you? How do you go on?" [2]

Up until that day I had managed to avoid reading *Moby Dick*. Walking back to the metro, I decided to rectify that and subsequently did. A copy now resides in the 'hallowed' section of the FPC library and is never too far from reach. There was also the strange delight of discovering some references to Fife in the book and a recent encounter with a building in the West Fife village of Limekilns caused me to search these out once again.

≈ ≈ ≈ ≈ ≈ ≈ ≈ ≈

Unlike a merchant vessel going from

point A > > > > > > > > > > > > > > > > > > to point B,

a whaling ship is prowling,

z   i   g   z

a

g

g

i

n

g

looking for prey.

≈ ≈ ≈ ≈ ≈ ≈ ≈ ≈

May 2013

The King's Cellar, as it is known today sits in the village of Limekilns just west of Rosyth. A more appropriate name would be "The Monk's Cellar" as the original building is believed to have been built by and for the monks of Dunfermline Abbey. The earliest official record of the building dates back to 1362, although the monks owned the surrounding Gellet lands as early as 1089 and it is believed that they used the "Vout" or "Vault" for storing wine and as a clearing house for monastic supplies brought in by sea. It is not clear when the building became known as the King's Cellar but is likely to be following the dissolution of the monasteries when it was no doubt appropriated by the Crown.

Today it almost appears as if the building is being sucked into the ground with the bottom windows almost at ground level.

High up in the trees

to the rear of the cellar

a buzzard (?)

Silent sentinel

bearing witness

observing our every move

as has always been done

The stone above the door is misleading as it bears the arms of the Pitcairn family and the date, 1581. Pitcairn owned part of Limekilns and was the King's private secretary and Commendator of Dunfermline. He lived in Limekilns and died in 1584, being buried in Dunfermline Abbey. The stone was transferred from his house.

Over the past 500 years the building has had parts of it rebuilt and adapted including the roof which was originally thatched. The building has been used as a wine cellar, storehouse, school, library, Episcopal Church in World War I, an air raid shelter in World War II. It is now used as a masonic lodge linked to the Bruce family of Robert the Bruce and the Elgin Marbles. A local belief exists that a secret underground tunnel connects the Cellar and the Palace at Dunfermline 4 miles away.

So what could be the connection of this building with Moby Dick?

Porpoises, indeed, are to this day considered fine eating. The meat is made into balls about the size of billiard balls, and being well seasoned and spiced might be taken for turtle-balls or veal balls. The old monks of

Dunfermline were very fond of them. They had a great porpoise grant from the crown.

From Chapter 65 of *Moby Dick* - The Whale as a Dish.

Is it too fanciful to imagine that this is the building where the porpoises would be landed for the old monks of Dunfermline?

Melville also quotes from Sibbald's *Fife and Kinross* in the first few pages of *Moby Dick:*

"Several whales have come in upon this coast (Fife). Anno 1652, one eighty feet in length of the whale-bone kind came in, which (as I was informed), besides a vast quantity of oil, did afford 500 weight of baleen. The jaws of it stand for a gate in the garden of Pitfirren."

From *Moby Dick* EXTRACTS (Supplied by a Sub-Sub-Librarian)

The reference to Pitfirren certainly refers to this locality and is now known as Pitfirrane, located just North West of Limekilns. I decided to have a look at Sibbald's original text which Melville used and discovered that the immediately preceding passage reads:

"There is a vast fond of small coal in the lands, which is carried to the port of Lyme Kills, belonging to Pitfirren [...] it is well provided with coal-yards and cellars. *Several whales have come in upon this coast..."*

Had Melville used the longer quote from Sibbald, Limekilns (as spelt today) would be mentioned in the book with a reference to cellars, albeit not the King's Cellar specifically.

There are a couple of other whaling references in Sibbald:

"The monks of Dunfermline had a grant from Malcolm IV of all the heads of a species of whale that should be caught in the Firth of Forth, (Scottwattre) but his Majesty reserved the most dainty bit to himself, viz. the tongue. It is curious to remark the revolutions of fashion in the article of eatables."

(Sibbald p. 116)

"There are several whales which haunt the Firth of Forth, which have fins or horny plates in the upper jaw, and most of them have spouts in their head; some of these are above seventy foot long, and some less: one of these with horny plates was stranded near to Bruntisland, (sic) which had no spout, but two nostrils like these of a horse. These whales with horny plates differ in the form of their snout, and in the number and form of their fins".

(Sibbald p. 117)

Two small paragraphs that offer a glimpse of a time passed, or has it? The privileges of royalty and the landed gentry arguably continue largely unabated and the non-human species of the globe decline to the point of extinction at the hands of the human actor.

There are many voices of Melville present in *Moby Dick* but one of them is clearly alerting humankind to pay attention and consider the consequences of potential ecological catastrophes arising from the lavish plunder of the natural world.

June 2013

Whilst out research is not conclusive by any means, we place a small photograph of Melville under the stones in front of the King's Cellar to secure the linkage in our own mind. When we pass this building in future, if nothing else, we will be reminded of Melville, Moby Dick and the King with a taste for cetacean tongues. And each time we see a copy of that encyclopedic text - *Moby Dick* - we will think of this small building in a West Fife village and of course Laurie Anderson who cast the line in our direction.

Now Playing: Laurie Anderson - *Life on a String*

20th June 2013

[1] Horsley

[2] Grogan

References:

Norman Fotheringham, *The Story of Limekilns* (Charlestown: Charlestown Lime Heritage Trust, 1997).

Molly Grogan, 'Laurie Anderson's Songs and Stories', *Paris Voice,* November 1999.

Carter B. Horsley, 'Songs and Stories from Moby Dick', *The City Review*, 5th October 1999.

Herman Melville, *Moby Dick or The Whale* (New York: Penguin Classics Edition, 1992).

Sir Robert Sibbald M. D., The History Ancient and Modern of the Sherrifdoms of Fife and Kinross (Cupar, Fife: R. Tullis, 1803).

Mike Zwerin, 'Laurie Anderson Grapples with Melville's Ghost' *The New York Times* 2nd December 1999.

Stalking the Shoreline

in fading light, at

cusp of sea and sky

barely a shadow, alone

stalking the shoreline

Now playing: Sun Kil Moon – *Heron Blue*

·

Searching for Storione - A Walk with the Ghosts of Little Moscow

Our research unit hasn't exactly excelled itself. A scribbled address on a torn piece of paper is all that we have:

Communist Literature Depot, 128 Perth Road, Cowdenbeath.

This is the only material link we have to Storione and even then we are not exactly sure of its provenance. Why does Goggle never come up with the really interesting stuff? It's a good job we still have some real libraries but further research can wait until our walk is over. We want to be open to the signs and an address is enough to get started...

~

We are taking a walk today from Lochgelly, via Lumphinnans, to Cowdenbeath in search of Lawrence Storione, founder of the Anarchist Communist League in 1908. We also intend our drift to act as a ritual exorcism of an article that 'British travel writer and humorist' Tim Moore wrote for the *Daily Telegraph* last year. His piece on Lochgelly and Cowdenbeath subsequently appeared in his book *You are Awful (but I Like You)*. What is curious about Moore's article is an almost complete lack of engagement with the actual materiality of this specific place. His encounters in pubs, hotels and fast food shops could have happened almost anywhere. (Just change the accents and place names).

Like anyone, Moore is entitled to respond to a place as he sees fit and after all he had a book to flog with a specific agenda: to visit the towns of 'unloved Britain'. Alongside Lochgelly and Cowdenbeath, Moore turns his c-list, Bill Bryson wit on the likes of Hull, Middlesbrough, Merthyr

Tydfil, Nottingham and Rhyl amongst others. The fact that this profound tome ended up in Richard Littlejohn's 'Best of 2012' year end list is probably all you need to know. "A laugh out loud pilgrimage to the most hideous places in modern Britain" says Littlejohn.

So, with regard to Cowdenbeath and Lochgelly, we can understand why he bothered to come, or did he? (How can you *not* find the football ground in Cowdenbeath?). There is just a slight suspicion that his article may have been written before he even arrived, just looking for some local colour to flesh out his prejudices. Not surprisingly, he 'found' what he was looking for which revolves around the fact that Lochgelly is routinely trotted out as the town having the cheapest housing prices in the UK.

The roads were lined with cramped little semis and 1960s bungalows, Britain's cheapest houses in their flimsy, pebbledashed glory.

All had the kind of scuffed and anonymous front door you could imagine a TV interviewer knocking upon at the end of a quest to track down some forgotten star of yesteryear.

"The Beirut of Fife"

Admittedly, Lochgelly, a mining town that has waxed and waned with the fortunes of the Fife coalfield may be quite a contrast to Mr Moore's birth town of Chipping Norton. Situated in the parliametary constituency of Witney, it is represented by one Mr David Cameron MP. (This is the stuff you can find on Google). Lochgelly's housing may also appear relatively cheap in comparison to the cost of Mr Moore's public school education. At 2012 prices a mere £16,035 per year per student. However, let's not be too harsh. A mildly humourous hack, hawking cheap laughs at the expense of a place ravaged by industrial decline is hardly worth fretting over. Oh and the word community is not mentioned once in Moore's article so he must be correct. The value of a place must be correlated to its house prices.

So we are off to take a walk and find out what this area says to us. As with *any* place we know that there will be stories embedded into the materiality of the buildings, spaces and the ground we walk on. They are out there in the sensory field and we are hopeful some of them may reveal themselves. This is an area that once returned Willie Gallacher as a Communist MP in the House of Commons from 1935 - 1950 and we have already mentioned Storione. Are all of these radical traces gone? Perhaps the ghosts of Little Moscow will reveal themselves to us. Will they have anything relevant to say to us in our present predicament? What of the future? Any insights will be gratefully received.

We convene at The Lochgelly Centre car park and it is a radiant, sun washed morning to set out. On a day like this Mr Moore could have taken himself down the road to experience one of Fife's outdoor gems: Lochore Meadows Country Park, or The Meedies as it is known locally. A fabulous public space and Outdoor Environmental Education Centre. Not being great respecters of chronological time our own despatch from the Meedies at an uncertain point in time can be found here.

The Lochgelly Centre, reopened last year after a major refurbishment. It's a fantastic community resource hosting a cafe, art exhibitions, various workshops and classes and a small theatre which hosts travelling companies and facilitates community arts projects. It also programmes film screenings, author readings such as Ian Rankin and Iain Banks and regularly hosts the perennials of the music gigging circuit. We can recall a slightly surreal chat one evening with Colin Blunstone and Rod Argent discussing The Zombies *Odyssey and Oracle*. We also saw a snarling Hugh Cornwall delivering one of his best post-Stranglers appearances that we've seen. These events happen in Lochgelly.

Anyway, we have barely stumbled a few steps from the car park when the ghosts start to whisper in our ears. Also located in the Lochgelly Centre is the Jennie Lee Library, named after one of Lochgelly's famous daughters. Jennie is keen to tell us two things: How a bursary helped a working class woman go to University and how open access was enshrined in her greatest achievement as Minister of the Arts, The Open University. At the time it was a genuinely radical idea that people could study for a university degree without having any initial qualifications at entry.

"The heroine of the whole story of the OU is Jennie Lee. The idea of it being called the Open University was very much hers"

Lord Asa Briggs

Jennie Lee was elected as an MP in 1929, becoming the youngest member of the House of Commons. Her maiden speech attacked Churchill's budget proposals which impressed him so much that he offered her his congratulations after their spirited exchange. Jennie maintained her independence of spirit and mind throughout her life clashing with her husband, Nye Bevan, on several policy issues, notably Bevan's support of the UK acquiring a nuclear deterrent which Jennie was firmly against.

Our encounter with Jennie Lee and the material presence of a library has already raised our spirits and by word association we recall another notable Lochgelly daughter Jennie Erdal, author of the fascinating memoir *Ghosting*.

Ghosting combines an account of her early childhood in Lochgelly and of her time employed as the ghostwriter for 'Tiger' a charismatic London-based publisher. Her ghostwriting assignments begin with personal letters, business correspondence and newspaper columns but, over time, eventually expand into novels and non-fiction titles. Whilst never named in Erdal's book, it is clear that 'Tiger' is Naim Attallah, owner of Quartet

Books, and for many years owner of *The Wire* - a music magazine dear to the hearts of the FPC. Our library also contains many fine Quartet titles including Arthur Taylor's *Notes and Tones* and Val Wilmer's *As Serious as Your Life* a ground breaking work on the post-Coltrane, jazz avant-garde. Funny how a walk in Lochgelly (not really even started yet!) has already taken us on a journey from Jennie Lee to Albert Ayler, Sun Ra and The AACM.

So with the sounds of saxophones ringing in our ears we can also eavesdrop in on a young, 14-year-old, miner's son picking up a sax for the first time. A birthday gift from an older brother, who played the trumpet.

Joe Temperley, places his fingers tentatively on the keys and blows to make his first sound. A sound that will initiate a journey that leads from Lochgelly to London, with Humphrey Lyttelton, and eventually over the Atlantic to New York and a stint with the Duke Ellington Orchestra.

With all this music ringing in our ears, we better be on our way and commence our drift up Bank Street. However, there must be something in the air today as we are soon distracted by a street sign. Could this be the definitive evidence that confirms Marc Bolan's debt to Chuck Berry? *Get it On* was supposedly adapted from Berry's *Little*  *Queenie* and here is the evidence: Berry straight to Bolan square(d).

Can you square a riff? We would like to think so.

As an aside, we had previously posted this photo on Twitter and off it went into the virtual ether. It soon returned like a digital boomerang with a note from *T.Rextasy - The World's Only Official Tribute to Marc Bolan and T Rex*. They have played Lochgelly Centre a number of times and had also noticed the sign but had never managed to take a photo.

Lochgelly's Bank Street/Main Street is the sort of place which capital has forgotten. In some ways this makes a refreshing change from the identikit, cloned high streets of more 'prosperous' towns full of the same old chain stores. There is a range of independent shops and a Co-op supermarket, which, despite its ethical credentials has been the subject of some disgruntled comments in the local press about high prices and abuse of their monopoly position. The buildings of Bank Street are solid and redolent of more prosperous days. The Cinema De-Luxe building, now a shop/office, retains a faded art-deco charm and you can transport yourself back to its luminous glory, offering up enticing wares of cinema, wrestling and dancing.

Around the corner, in Main Street stands the recently restored and still magnificent Miners Institute.

This building is now used as the Fife Women's Technology Centre, an award winning community based learning centre that has been providing training in new technology to unemployed women since 1990.

Next door is the new Ore Valley Business Centre a state-of-the-art business centre aimed at helping start-up businesses in Fife to grow. The building has been designed to be highly energy-efficient, maximising solar gain and environmental management technology to keep the building's energy requirements to a minimum.

In these two buildings alone is evidence of some of the good work going on to improve Lochgelly today and build towards the future. Like many of the towns and villages around this area, they prospered with the deep mining of the Fife coalfield but suffered disproportionately when the industry began to decline and was eventually delivered a terminal bullet from the Thatcher government. We are reminded of Patrick Geddes's inter-linked triad of Place Work and Folk. Is it any wonder that when 'work' is withdrawn, almost wholesale from an area, Place and Folk suffer?

At the side of the Miners Institute is a sculpture called *The Prop* by the celebrated artist David Annand. Annand's other many notable works includes the statue of poet Robert Fergusson, outside the Canongate Church in Edinburgh, and <u>*Turfman*</u>, a collaboration with Seamus Heaney.

The Prop portrays a lone miner propping up, or holding on, to six stainless steel forms, representing pit props? A reminder of the town's mining heritage but an addition to a new sense of place in its own right. This is not monumental art. It quietly invites you to spend time with it. Walk around the space to catch the light fracturing off of the shining stainless forms and it's then you notice that each column has a line of poetry engraved in to it. We subsequently learn that the poem *God is a Miner* is by local poet William Hershaw.

The miner looks as if he has just emerged from a coal seam, rough-hewn from deep time. Absorbing light into solid form in contrast to the sleek, reflective stainless steel.

~

"The radicalism of Little Moscow developed out of a struggle to maintain and improve the basic conditions of life."

Stuart MacIntyre

We now heading down the long ribbon strip that connects Lochgelly with Cowdenbeath but is actually called Lumphinnans. There is housing down the north side of the road and an impressive cryptoforest to the south with a golf course beyond. Were you to pass through this area today it may not be immediately apparent that this was once the beating heart of Little Moscow. An area that elected Willie Gallacher, a Communist, as Member of Parliament for West Fife from the period 1935 - 1950.

Little Moscow was a term applied to a small number of towns and villages in the UK that appeared to hold extreme left-wing political values. In Scotland there was Lumphinnans and Vale of Leven, England had Chopwell and there was Maredy in Wales. The term was initially used as a term of disparagement by the popular press but then reclaimed as a 'badge of honour' by the local communities. Many of the areas that would later be dubbed 'Little Moscows' had earlier in the century attempted to find alternatives to the state sanctioned capitalist system.

In Lumphinnans, one of the key instigators was Lawrence Storione who arrived in the village in 1908. Storione was born in Italy in 1867 in the French-speaking area of Valle d'Aosta and later worked as a miner. It appears that he was introduced to anarchism by the noted French geographer and anarchist Élisée Reclus, who was lecturing at the University of Brussels. (Incidentally, Elisee and his brother Élie were friends of Patrick Geddes and attended Geddes's International Summer Schools in Edinburgh, as did Peter Kropotkin). Due to his anarchist activities, Storione was forced to flee France disguised as a woman and he arrived in Scotland in 1897, working in the mines of Ayrshire and Lanarkshire. After an aborted trip to Canada he returned to Scotland in 1908 where he settled in Lumphinnans and took up employment at the No 1 pit. His arrival at Lumphinnans had consequences for revolutionary ideas among the miners in that area and he soon set up the Anarchist Communist League which, according to Stuart MacIntyre: "preached a heady mixture of De Leonist Marxism and the anarchist teachings of Kropotkin and Stirner." Among those who appeared to have joined the League were the miners Abe and Jim Moffat and Robert (Bob) Selkirk. All three were to join the Communist Party in 1922, Abe Moffat having an important position within it and Selkirk serving as a Communist Party town councillor in Cowdenbeath for 24 years. The League set up a bookshop in 1916 in nearby Cowdenbeath at 128 Perth Road - which is where we are headed today. It sold titles such as Kropotkin's *Mutual Aid*, Stirner's *The Ego and His Own*, and De Leon's *Two Pages From Roman History* and other anarchist literature.

Storione married Annie Cowan in 1900 and their children could only grow into their names: Armonie, Anarchie, Autonomie, Germinal and Libertie! The sole exception to these revolutionary appellations was his daughter Annie who was a leading light in a Proletarian Sunday School in Cowdenbeath. Sunday evening meetings were held at which notable activists such as Willie Gallacher, John McLean, and Jack Leckie came to speak.

It's an enjoyable walk in the sunshine and it looks like a straight road towards Cowdenbeath, unbroken by housing when as if out of nowhere we are forced to drift from the main road by a sign:

A small road leads off to the right and in seconds, our landscape has completely changed. An open road stretches out ahead with spectacular vistas over to Benarty Hill and The Bishop. Old style telegraph poles whistling in the light wind appear to be humming a chorus of Wichita Lineman and we wonder whether we have stepped through a portal to the American mid-west.

Our thoughts of Franco-Italian anarchists are derailed for a while until we recall the high correlation between anarchists and geographers. The land has always been important to the anarchist.

We subsequently come across the story of Lumphinnans NoXI mine which we guess was North West from here and was called the Peeweep pit as the miners could always hear the sound of Lapwings as they walked to work.

We also add to our collection of single-item, lost footwear.

After our detour we are looking for any signs that remain of Little Moscow. The most obvious traces are to be found in the street signs: Gagarin Way and Gallacher Place.

Named after Yuri Alekseyevich Gagarin, the first human to journey into outer space and hero of the Soviet Union.

This street also gave the name to Gregory Burke's debut play which is perhaps a useful corrective to avoid becoming too nostalgic and romantic about institutionalised, political rhetoric of any persuasion.

We invoke the ghosts to tell us anything that may be of use to us. Rather than deliver any political sloganeering Willie Gallagher tells us a story, or more like a scene from a play. It concerns the incident of a 12 year old girl brought before the Communist baillie, Jimmie Stewart for stealing a bag of coal:

Stewart: How auld are ye lassie?

Girl: Just twal sir

Stewart: How auld is yer wee brother?

Girl: He's eight

Stewart: It was gey cauld last week?

Girl: Aye, it was gey cauld

Stewart: Did ye take the coal hen?

Girl: Aye

Stewart: Muckle?

Girl: Just a bucketful

Stewart: Did ye take the coal to make a fire for your wee brother?

Girl: Aye

Stewart: What ye did was richt. Charge dismissed. (1)

A more postmodern take on street names can be found with Robert Smith Court. Anyone spending time in the towns an villages of West Fife will notice that there a large number of pubs called The Goth. (after The Gothenburg System). It therefore only appears fitting that there should exist a commemoration of the uber-goth himself in this street sign. We are surprised that it has not become more of a shrine. Perhaps a few stuffed, cuddly *Love Cats* would be appropriate although, there is the small beginnings of *A Forest*.*

We have almost reached Cowdenbeath, when another sign whispers to us:

The WEA (Workers' Educational Association) was founded in 1903 and is the UK's largest voluntary sector provider of adult education. In many ways it was a forerunner of the Open University.

We are transported to last years summer holiday when we visited the Hepworth Gallery in Wakefield. Showing alongside Richard Long's artist room was Luke Fowler's film: *The Poor Stockinger, The Luddite Cropper and the Deluded Followers of Johanna Southcott.*

Fowler's film focuses on the work of historian E.P. Thompson, who was employed by the WEA to teach literature and social history to adults in the industrial towns of the West Riding of Yorkshire. Like the Open University this was an opportunity to provide classes to people who had historically been unable to access a university education.

The film uses archive and contemporary footage to portray a moment of optimism in which E.P. Thompson's ideas for progressive education came together with a West Riding tradition of political resistance and activism. In many ways you can feel the bonds of solidarity stretching from the Little Moscow of Fife to the West Riding of Yorkshire.

And so we reach Cowdenbeath and it's not too difficult to locate Perth Road. 128 is what our scribbled piece of paper says. Will there be any sign from Storione?

It's not looking too hopeful as it soon becomes clear that the buildings are residential terraced houses probably built in the 1960s/70s. We soon track down No 128 although there is no obvious trace of The Communist Literature Depot having existed.

The calendars does not measure time as clocks do. They are monuments of a historical consciousness of which not the slightest trace has been apparent in the past hundred years.

A historian [...] stops telling the sequence of events like the beads of a rosary. Instead he grasps the constellation which his own era has formed with a definite earlier one. Thus he establishes a conception of the present as the 'time of now' which is shot through with chips of Messianic time.

Walter Benjamin, *Theses on the Philosophy of History*

Perhaps it is enough to know that Storione's bookshop may have once existed here and now resides within this little collective of numbers. A radiating form of energy that once rippled through the ether of Little Moscow and now lies awaiting its Messianic moment.

Tim who?

~ ~ ~

Now Playing: Dick Gaughan - *A Handful of Earth*

25th May 2013

(1) This is an actual transcript recorded in Stuart MacIntyre's book.

* The real Robert Smith was also a Communist councillor and appears to have suggested the proposal to name Gagarin Way.

References:

Walter Benjamin, 'Theses on the Philosophy of History', 1940, in Tasmin Spargo, (ed), *Reading the Past* (London: Palgrave, 2000).

Nick Heath, *Lawrence Storione 1867 - 1922,* on Libcom.org: *http://libcom.org/history/storione-lawrence-1867-1922*

William Kenefick, *Red Scotland! The Rise and Fall of the Radical Left*, c. 1872 to 1932 (Edinburgh: Edinburgh University Press, 2007).

Stuart Macintyre, *Little Moscows: Communism and working-class militancy in inter-war Britain* (London: Croom Helm, 1980).

Tim Moore, *You Are Awful (But I Like You): Travels Through Unloved Britain* (London: Jonathan Cape, 2012).

Neil C. Rafeek, *Communist Women in Scotland: Red Clydeside from the Russian Revolution to the End of the Soviet Union* (London: I.B. Tauris, 2008).

Footfall Democracy - Desire Line

d

   e

      s

     l   i   n   e

         r

         e

Dunfermline

29th October 2014

Worlds within Worlds

                in

                worlds

wor ds

                    or

wor   ds

            in

worl   ds

            o ld

wor ds

        thin

            worlds

worlds within worlds

from the ocean

land forms

islands

an archipelago

of weather

and time

telescope, or

microscope?

thin world portal,

sea or sky?

an autarky

of green

only open

to sun

and rain

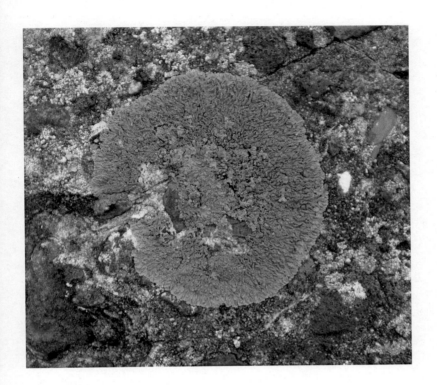

the high lands

shape

invisible cities

littoral drift

lagoon

an oxbow lake

The Charlestown limeworks were one of the earliest industrial complexes in Scotland at the advent of the industrial revolution. Conceived in 1752, within ten years, they had become the largest lime producing facility in Europe.

The Charlestown limestone was quarried locally. Coral laid down 300 million years ago formed calcium carbonate (limestone) which was heated in the kilns with coal to 900°C. During this process the weight of stone reduced by 40%. More of a devils' share than an angels' share.

Working conditions have been described as a "hellish scene" with the hot air thick with sulphur and ammonia from the limeburning. The list of worker's functions leach from the page into the 'old words':

Kilnheadman

Drawer

Trimmer

Slaker

Emptier

Sawyer

Mason

Wright

Labourer

Overseer

Today the kilns exist as another, largely, forgotten memory of an industrial past. The encroaching green fingers are tightening their grip.

on the old railway track

traces of sleeping

sleepers

above the surface

vertical calm

conceals

unseen networks

of rhizomatic agitation

On Charlestown Brae

the old horse trough

a flowering

of water and air

the need to create, islands for contemplation.

≈

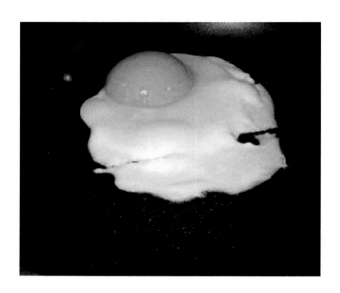

Heat formed

in black ocean

a coastline emerges.

Inlets, an isthmus

white tundra,

transmuted gold.

≈

From a short walk in Charlestown, Fife.

Now playing: Steve Roden - *Four Possible Landscapes*.

24th October 2014

Reference:

Norman Fotheringham, *Charlestown, Built on Lime* (Charlestown: Charlestown Lime Heritage Trust, 1997).

Tidal Flux

Worlds with - in worlds

tidal

flux   in

Firth of Forth

Now playing: Chris Abrams / Mike Cooper - 'Memory of Water' (from *Oceanic Feeling - Like*)

30th July 2014

Silverburn: in the Flux and Flow of Place

We are walking out, along the shoreline, from Leven towards Lundin Links. Coastal energies are in full flow, our field of vision filled with an excess of sand, sea and sky.

In the distance, an intensity of white light appears to drift in the Firth of Forth like a frosted iceberg. The Bass Rock. Invisible threads loop in the conical forms of Berwick Law and the sacred hill of Largo Law. Three nodes of a triangle that collapse North and South; earth and water; land and sky. An energy field that pulls us into an expanded world. Bardic bird yells, brine on the tongue and buffeting sea breezes whip up folding white breakers that fizz over the sand.

≈

We soon encounter the talisman lying in the dunes. It's protective, synthetic membrane, perished long ago by wind and water. Now crusted with sand and water-logged, it has transmuted into a living entity. Green tendrils sprout from the surface. It appears to be an auspicious omen, a process of alchemy worthy of the legendary Wizard of Balwearie, Michael Scot, (1175 – c.1232), reputed to have form in these parts.

Local legend has it that Scot summoned his three imp familiars, Prig, Prim and Pricker to Largo Law with a view to levelling it. A sort of job creation scheme for hyper-active familiars. As they began to dig, Scot had a change of plan and the imps were hurriedly despatched to Kirkcaldy to make ropes out of sand. This was to assist Scot in his showdown with the devil on Kirkcaldy beach. Scot appears to have triumphed in the encounter as evidenced by a local saying: "The devil's dead and buried in Kirkcaldy". As a result of the 'Kirkcaldy interruption', only a single shovelful of earth was thrown from Largo Law to create the cairn of Norrie's Law at the wonderfully named farm of Baldastard. There are also local folk tales about an abundant goldmine that supposedly exists underneath Largo Law and that sheep have returned from grazing on the foothills with golden fleeces.

≈

Giant stepping-stones. Largo Law ahead.

Huge concrete blocks line this part of the coast like giant stepping-stones. Could we step all the way to Largo Law? The blocks were part of the necklace of coastal defences installed during WW2 and were designed to frustrate any German tank invasion from the sea. The blocks were constructed and laid by the Polish army who had several divisions based in Fife during WW2. Today, the original purpose of the blocks may be somewhat forgotten but their solidity and mass provide a pleasing sculptural rhythm to the foreshore.

One of the blocks serves as a makeshift altar to revere the action of the natural world on our talismanic old football. A process of transmutation - of rebirth and growth.

We turn inland from the coast to take the path, called Mile Dyke, that heads between the links golf courses. This will take us to Silverburn and we can now feel its connection to Leven and the coast. S i l v e r - b u r n is a name to roll around the mouth and along with golden fleeces and transmuted footballs we can sense that we are truly in an alchemical landscape.

≈

Silverburn - a Brief History

Silverburn is the former estate of The Russell family who were owners of the Tullis Russell paper making business. The land was originally part of the Barony of Durie and was leased to Mr David Russell by Charles Maitland Christie of Durie in 1854. Arthur Russell purchased the land in 1866 and rebuilt Silverburn House. A dower house known as Corriemar was also built and a flax mill was established on the site.

David Russell died in 1906. His son, (also named David) and who later became Sir David Russell was born at Silverburn in 1872 and in 1912 married and went to live in Aithernie House. He returned to Silverburn in 1929. Sir David had a great interest in trees and many were planted including some rare and unusual species which continue to thrive today.

The flax mill closed around 1930.

In 1973, Sir David Russell's grandson, Major Russell (Head of Tullis Russell Paperworks) gifted the houses and grounds to Leven Town Council, but also stipulated through the National Trust for Scotland that the "subjects should remain forever as a quiet area used for the benefit of the public in general and the people of Leven in particular for nature trails, quiet parkland and organised camping". In the mid to late 1980s, the former Kirkcaldy District Council undertook a Job Creation Programme to reinstate Silverburn House for use as a Residential Centre for groups to use such as scouts and guides; school parties, caravan rallies etc. A stand-alone wing to the rear of the House was used by crafters to make and show their wares throughout the Summer and Christmas/New Year periods.

Between 1990 and 1999, an average of 20,000 + people per year visited Silverburn. Its main attraction was the former "Mini-Farm" which had on show a wide range of domestic and exotic animals, birds, reptiles and insects. However, following a Council policy decision in 2002, to cease operating Animal Centres across Fife there have been very few visitors to Silverburn, other than local people. Financial constraints have also led to year-on-year reductions in revenue expenditure with no meaningful capital investment in the Park.

Over the years, various ideas have been proposed for Silverburn including the setting up of a Scottish Music/Arts and Craft Centre and redevelopment as a crematorium. None of these have come to fruition.

However, work is presently underway by Fife Employment Access Trust ("FEAT") in collaboration with the local community, agencies and local authorities in the Levenmouth area on a project entitled 'Heart Mind Soul Silverburn'. This aim of this initiative is to secure a long-term future for the park and to promote wellbeing and employment opportunities.

≈

We have visited Silverburn a number of times over the past few months. Drifting around the mixed woodland trails and environs of the estate at different times, on different days and in different weather conditions. Most apparent is observing and feeling the subtle changes of a thriving natural world; an incipient wildness forever encroaching on the deteriorating materiality of the buildings. Silverburn is a place highly conducive to the immersive dérive. A locus of past, present and possible.

≈

The excellent Blacketyside Farm Shop is a wonderful place for sustenance at the start or finish of a Silverburn visit. However, this does means crossing the A915 road which is the main artery into the East Neuk of Fife. The road is a long, straight stretch which can be very busy with vehicles tanking past at high-speed:

wheeeeeeeeeeeeeeeeeejjjjjjjjjjjjjjjjjjggrooooooooooooooooooooom

mmmmmm oi nnnnnnnnnnnn

nnnnnnnnnnnn oi mmmmmm

mmmmmm oi nnnnnnnnnnnn

wheeeeeeeeeeeeeeeeeejjjjjjjjjjjjjjjjjjggrooooooooooooooooooooom

≈

Enter Silverburn

Overhead, a charcoal smudged blue heralds a chorus of rooks riffing off the traffic screech.

Giant American redwoods stand sentinel, stretching for the sun. "Ambassadors from another time" silently announcing that this may not be your conventional Scottish woodland:

The redwoods, once seen, leave a mark or create a vision that stay with you always. No one has ever successfully painted or photographed a redwood tree. The feeling they produce is not transferable. From them comes silence and awe. It's not only their unbelievable stature, nor the

colour which seems to shift and vary under your eyes, no, they are not like any trees we know, they are ambassadors from another time.

John Steinbeck

N: "do you know you can punch a redwood and it doesn't hurt your hand?"

Blue melts to green as sunlight showers through the tree canopy, dappling the forest floor. Traffic thrum gradually dissolves in the low lipping burr of the flowing burn. A sunken path beckons and so our immersion into Silverburn begins.

Once in the shade, a sprinkling of light and water; a scattering of silver drops:

 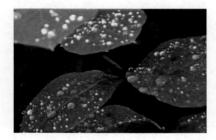

A network of wooded paths through and around Silverburn provide ample scope for aimless drifting. The topography is interesting with a long flat elevated plateau where Silverburn House sits which tumbles away quite steeply down to the flax mill with the golf courses and coast beyond.

Depending which path you take you will soon stumble across one of the ghosts...

≈

Corriemar: The Dower House

Corriemar is thought to have been the dower house for Silverburn House. A dower house is usually a moderately large house available for use by the widow (dowager) of the estate-owner.

Corriemar has been vacant since 1970, having previously served as day patient accommodation for Stratheden Hospital or the Fife and Kinross District Asylum as it was formerly known. (Stratheden will be a place-name that resides in the (un)consciousness of many Fifers. My mother used to say that the teenage antics of my brother and I would send her there. In hindsight, I hope that she was only joking. RIP Mum).

The house today is a crumbling ghost of a building. Buildings need capital, care and a purpose to thrive and Corriemar has had neither of these since the 1970s. Now officially classified as a dangerous building and on the Buildings at Risk register, nature is slowly restaking her claim.

A pine tree grows out of the roof guttering. Many slate tiles have been lost to the elements, leaving the roof like a mouth full of smashed teeth.

The building is not just boarded but sealed.

Mute.

All flow and circulation broken:

Graffiti abhors a blank surface and Corriemar has become a canvas for a surprisingly diverse display:

Interesting in that all of these shots, the green leaves of nature always encroach into the frame.

Silverburn House

Once a home to the Russell family. Old, super-8 film shows children playing and running around on the lawn in front of the house. Adults relax in deck chairs, smoking and chatting...

Now, like Corriemar, Silverburn House is sealed up and dangerous:

Broken Flows:

The entrance to the old crafts centre:

Stretching for the sky:

On our last visit, we noticed a new addition. Some outdoor seating has been added, fashioned out of tree trunks:

And at the opposite end of the lawn, a collection of shamanistic divining posts in the family sculpture area:

As is common with any drift, with a little attention, a surreal world can reveal itself:

The shoe tree:

The worm mound:

One tries to wriggle free:

The giant pencil:

The stalled roundabout:

The unknown and undecipherable signs:

≈

One visit, late Saturday afternoon, a dull twilight. No other humans around and even the bird song is subdued. Only the rustle of leaves - hopping blackbird and scurrying rabbit. The fungi radiate a pale light:

A message from the trees:

Stare for long enough and the tree spirits begin to reveal themselves:

Tusked boar

dog-bear

Cyclops   Preying Mantis

tentacle clawed ... ?

≈

The Flax Mill & Retting Pond

On the lower level of Silverburn sits the Flax Mill and its associated retting pond.

Retting is a process which employs the action of micro-organisms and moisture on plants to dissolve or rot away much of the cellular tissues and pectins surrounding bast-fibre bundles. This process is used in the production of fibre from plant materials such as flax and hemp stalks and coir from coconut husks.

The flax mill was built in the mid-1800s and was one of the first industrial buildings to be roofed with a 'new material' called corrugated iron. Flax fibre was prepared for spinning at Silverburn and was soaked in the retting ponds for about 10 days, after which it was thrashed. Retting Ponds were brought into play after an Act in 1806 prohibited the use of local streams due to excessive pollution which occurred from the process. The flax mill itself was run on steam power. The mill closed in 1930, although, as previously mentioned, the outbuildings were used for the mini zoo during the 1990s. Today, the brickwork is failing in some places, with over 50% of the brick turned to dust. An adjacent row of cottages were probably built for the flax mill workers and remain used and in good condition today.

Look out for the face in the factory:

and the quizzical ghost:

The outbuildings:

The old stables:

Inside the old stable

the darkest corners - bleed

in slatted sunlight

The retting pond where the flax was soaked is close by. Now heavily overgrown with vegetation, it is a meditative spot to watch the reflected trees in the water and the teeming pond life on the surface:

≈

The Tree House and Formal Gardens

How could anyone not be captivated by the tree house? It looks as if it could walk away at any moment on its stilted legs:

The sense of being watched by the animal heads on either side add a touch of the uncanny:

By complete coincidence, N has a copy of *Reforesting Scotland* in his bag. The cover illustration an echo of what we are standing underneath:

The formal gardens, also comprise a sensory and walled garden. They are clearly places of meaning and memory. On our first visit, we find a wreath of knitted flowers:

By the time of our second visit they have gone. There are also the lives commemorated and remembered. Emotional linkages between people and place.

From the sensory garden, the gentle trickle of running water projects around the natural amphitheatre. Bees congregate upon yellow and pink petals shower down on grey.

Perhaps there is also evidence of the cunning folk at play. A small entrance through a hedge; a portal to another world?

≈

What is in a Name?

We leave Silverburn to head for the coast once again. Following the flow of the burn back down Mile Dyke to where the silver stream meets the sea.

We reflect on the name:

Silver - precious, with, the highest conductivity of any metal, allowing energy to flow.

Burn - always in flux/flow. As Heraclitus said, you never step in the same river twice and we know we will never visit the same Silverburn twice. There is also the idea of how prescribed burning of vegetation can recycle nutrients tied up in old plant growth to invigorate new growth. With the current FEAT and community initiative 'Heart Mind Soul Silverburn' perhaps new possibilities for Silverburn are emerging.

And to end. A whispered message from a beach encounter:

≈

To end with a name and only the name. To end with only the letters of the name:

Silver sun sliver -

burrs liven us.

River veils runes
in blue siren lures.

Briers line ruins,
burn rises in
river lens.

Vein in burn
silver in vein
burn silver
S i l v e r b u r n.

Now playing: The Necks – *Silverwater*

26th September 2013

References:

Buildings at Risk Register for Scotland

County Folk-Lore Vol VII. Examples of Printed Folk-Lore concerning Fife with some notes on Clackmannan and Kinross-Shires collected by John Ewart Simpkins (London: Sidgwick & Jackson for the Folk-Lore Society, 1914).

RCHAMS, Canmore

John Steinbeck, *Travels with Charley: In Search of America*. (New York: Viking, 1962).

Marysia Lachowicz, *Polish Army in Fife*. (Work in Progress).

With very special thanks to Margaret and Aiveen for the invitation to "come and see what we make of it" and also Aiveen, Margaret, Graham and Ninian for inspiration and sharing that first visit.

Echoes of the Pioneers: Three Beehives in Leven

Walk up Durie Street in Leven and listen out for the bees singing. Perhaps, the sound of the skep is more of a muted murmur now, but raise your eyes from street level and you may hear them.

The first hive is above what is now the town library. Our industrious and co-operative little bees swarm around their skep as they have done since 1887.

This symbolic image on a former building of the Leven Reform Co-operative Society reminds us of the Rochdale Pioneers. In 1844, with an economy in decline, wage reductions and strikes, a group of unemployed weavers met at the Socialist Institute to debate the philosophies of Robert Owen and Chartism. Whilst there are many examples of co-operative societies existing before 1844, The Rochdale Pioneers formulated a set of guiding principles, upon which, an expansive version of co-operation was founded. Looking at these principles today, it is notable how well these stand up as a set of co-operative ideals:

1. Democratic control, one member one vote and equality of the sexes.

2. Open membership.

3. A fixed rate of interest payable on investment.

4. Pure, unadulterated goods with full weights and measures given.

5. No credit.

6. Profits to be divided pro-rata on the amount of purchase made (the dividend or divi).

7. A fixed percentage of profits to be devoted to educational purposes.

8. Political and religious neutrality.

The Rochdale Society of Equitable Pioneers raised money from 28 original subscribers to establish a shop at 31 Toad Lane, Rochdale which was equipped and stocked with basic goods and produce. The Pioneers chose the beehive as a symbol of co-operation and unity and the original stone skep stood on top of the, now demolished, central store at 45-51 Toad Lane, Rochdale. The skep now sits preserved and incorporated into the outside wall of the Rochdale Pioneers museum.

Within ten years of the Pioneers founding efforts the co-operative movement in Britain had grown to nearly 1,000 co-operatives with many adopting the symbol of the beehive.

We are back in Leven. Follow the echoes and walk further up Durie Street. On the clock of the former Co-operative department store, a golden skep, clotting the fingers of weak, ebbing sunlight:

Stand. Raise your head and look to the sky. Follow the thread of sibilant hum to the very top of the building. A change of tone - to low dissonant drone. A sign that the bees are, once again, getting ready to swarm:

110

Underneath the skep
intimations of new life
still sounding - echoes
of the Pioneers.

Now Playing: Earth - The Bees Made Honey In The Lion's Skull
12th September 2013
References:
The Rochdale Pioneers Museum
Manchester History

Found Totem

Found totem

Forest clearing

Now playing: The Sarsen Circle - The Sarsen Circle (Live)

17th April 2014

The Wild Wood

Beyond the hawthorn, lies the wild wood

"cuckoo, cuckoo"

over the threshold
forms and colours
of the Otherworld

... snake-eye stirs

jaw click, snout
and a slither
of tongues

threat or supplication?
paw or claw?
who hears the cry
of the wild wood?

No one here
anyone?

the oracle
of the wood
whispers:

... always the leaves

... always the light

≈ ≈ ≈

Hawthorn bushes and the call of a cuckoo conjure up the tale of Thomas the Rhymer a thirteenth century Scottish mystic, wandering minstrel and poet. Folklore tells of how Rhymer meets the Faery Queen by a hawthorn bush from which a cuckoo is calling. The Queen takes Rhymer on a journey of forty days and forty nights to enter the faery underworld. Some versions of the tale say Rhymer was in the underworld for a brief sojourn. Others say for seventy years, after becoming the Queen's consort. Eventually, Rhymer returns to the mortal world where he finds he has been absent for seven years. The theme of travellers being waylaid by faery folk and taken to places where time passes faster or slower are common in Celtic mythology. The hawthorn is one of the most likely trees to be inhabited or protected by the faery folk.

The wild wood can be found amongst the terra incognita of farmland, old paths and hedgerows between the village of Pattiesmuir and Dunfermline, Fife.

Now playing: Bert Jansch - 'The Tree Song' from *Birthday Blues*.

13th July 2014

Dunfermline Linen Co.

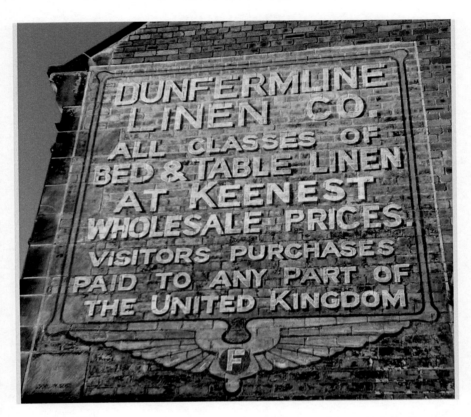

Restored ghost sign in New Row Dunfermline. Does this now make it a sign haunted by a ghost sign?

Now Playing: Triosk - *Moment Returns*

16th January 2013

When Natural Cycles Turn, Brutalist Windows Can Dream of Trees...

a flower expresses itself by flowering, not by being labelled

Patrick Geddes

That blue
There - beyond the iris heads.
As if a grey tarpaulin
has been peeled back
across the eyeball of the sky.

Spring light, a different light.

Colours made strange,
as smears of white heat
dab at fold-gathered shadows.

The spooling thread of a blackbird's raga, weaves through a chitter-chatter tapestry of blue tit and sparrow song as we lie under the flowers, observing a line of marching ants. A posse of advance troops, jolted into collective industry after winter's hibernation. Out, once again, to prospect and survey the land.

Here. Now. All of us. Feeling the natural cycles turn.

Looking up to the sky from underneath the flowers.

An ant's world view invoking vague memories of *Land of the Giants,* and of this place before the flowers arrived.

Across the road, jump the fence and head towards what turns out to be a picture frame.

Walking into the frame and down an avenue of young trees, we are lured by the vanishing point of reflecting silver.

Flocks of daffodils gather around the rotunda, a yellow flecked congregation. Heads nodding, as if worshipping the filigree forms of a newly descended alien god. Bringer of light and heat.

A turn into mature woodland and a network of tracks and paths. A sense of water running close-by but which we cannot see - yet. Tree animism.

You will have to move closer,

to hear,

the guttural whispers

of the tree maw

With spring sunshine, woodland, birdsong and the sense of water, this feels like 'the countryside' but it doesn't take long to be reminded how close we are to the centre of this New Town. We look up at the polished concrete belly of transport entrails as the low thrum of traffic passes overhead.

In the last photograph, on the left hand side, you can see what turns out to be a rather incongruous plinth nestling under the concrete flyover. We discover that it is displaying a 16th century stone-carved coat of arms, of the Leslie family. The stone originally came from an old building in the nearby policies (grounds) of Leslie House, the ancestral home of the Earls of Rothes. It bears the griffins and motto of the Leslie family: *Grip Fast*

From Kinross, I came to Lessley, where I had a full view of the palace of Rothess, both inside and outside ... The house is the glory of the place and indeed of the whole province of Fife.

Daniel Defoe, 1724

Sir Norman Leslie acquired Fythkil, the original name of this parish, around 1282 and renamed it after the Rothes family lands in Aberdeenshire. The Leslies became the Earls of Rothes in 1457. The earliest evidence of a house on this site is 1667 which was destroyed by fire in December 1763. A much smaller house was subsequently built, supposedly restoring the least damaged Western side.

The Earls of Rothes, obviously didn't *Grip Fast* enough as we soon alight on the ancestral home, now sealed off with iron spiked fencing. It's not too difficult to find a way in to have a quick look. The building looks fairly structurally sound but is minus a roof and much of the interior, creating the effect of being able to see right through the facade to the other side.

One part of the fabric that has clearly survived intact is the flagpole which we can see through various windows:

In.

Spring light

No flags fly

≈

To the left of the house are a tiered set of south-facing terraces, although now denuded of any plant life other than the carefully manicured grass. Like the grounds in front of the house it shows that some care and maintenance is obviously still taking place ...

Whilst, in the conservatory, the buddleia appears to be thriving:

We are just about to scale the wall that will take us to the front of the house when we hear voices on the other side and decide to exit the grounds quietly by the way we came in.

We subsequently learn that the house had been acquired by Sir Robert Spencer Nairn in 1919 who, supposedly, as he saw the advancing development of the New Town, gifted it to the Church of Scotland in 1952 for use as an Eventide Home. After falling into disuse, the house was sold for property development in 2005. Little appears to have happened until December 2009 when an unexplained 'raging inferno' reduced the property to its present state.

≈

We head down towards the River Leven, thinking of its flowing waters coursing through the Fife landscape from Loch Leven near Kinross all the way to joining the Firth of Forth at Leven. What memory does this water hold? Of powering linen mills and the local paper mills of Tullis Russell and Smith Anderson. Of sustaining the tadpoles and sticklebacks in the pond where we used to peer into the depths searching for those tiny flickering tails. The webbed feet of the white swans gliding through the water today.

Before heading down to the riverside, we stop to listen to the bridge. The wind plucked treble of the harp like strings:

... and the deep base drones of the underside sound box. We expect the huge columnar legs to start lumbering forward at any time:

As always, the eaves of the bridge have been tagged.

Power and capital, enabled The Leslie family to appropriate, name and tag these lands. Our graffiti artist(s) tag is of a more existentialist nature. "I am here, in this place".

Following the course of the river, this world becomes a little stranger when we encounter the hippos traversing their water hole:

A familiar encounter in this town. If Proust had his madeleine to kick him into paroxysms of involuntary memory, then the image of a hippo should do the trick for anyone who grew up in this town.

It's not just the hippos. It's also the dinosaurs, henges, flying saucers, pipe tunnels, giant hands, the toadstools and other curios which all 'do something' to social space for those who stumble across them.

Two bin bags murmur in agreement as they huddle in the shade, underneath the clatter of skateboards, waiting for the sun to come around.

Ascending the hill to the town centre, we are reminded that every place needs its temples

And what would any New Town be without its Brutalist municipal buildings? Guaranteed to be derided as 'plooks', 'carbuncles' and in this case, contributing to its award as 'the most dismal town in Britain 2009'.

Well, perhaps it's all a matter of perspective and the warm fingers of spring weather but the buildings are looking far from dismal today.

Tactile, concrete carpets, frame frozen flight and light.

Frozen flight - open sky

The original Brutalist grey cube of Fife House with its newer postmodern counterpart. It has to be a grandfather clock?

Green detailing can soften even the most austere facade:

Whilst brutalist windows, can dream of trees and sky.

Nearby, North facing Rothesay house hasn't weathered quite as well.

After a walk back down to the public park, with vistas to the Paps of Fife we almost return to our starting point. Layers of place intersecting with past present and future in the returning bright light of Spring.

We nod to the defenceless one as we pass.

Comforted that the Good Samaritan is looking on from not too far away

And, as we leave town, how can we not stop to take delight in the toadstools. Vibrant and colourful, they look as if they have just (re)emerged, stretching into the returning Spring light.

Their months quietly growing in winter darkness appear to have passed.

≈

Now Playing: Motorpsycho - *Behind the Sun*.

17th April 2014

Note:

The New Town is Glenrothes in Fife. Planned in the late 1940s as one of Scotland's first post-second world war new towns, its original purpose was to house miners who were to work at a newly established state-of the-art coal mine, the Rothes Colliery. The mine never opened commercially and the town subsequently became an important part of Scotland's emerging electronics industry 'Silicon Glen'. It is now the administrative capital of Fife.

Glenrothes was the first town in the UK to appoint a town artist in 1968. This is now recognised as playing a significant role, both in a Scottish and in an international context, in helping to create the idea of art being a key factor in creating a sense of place. Two town artists, David Harding (1968–78) and Malcolm Roberston (1978–91), were employed supported by a number of assistants, including Stan Bonnar who created the hippos. A large variety of artworks and sculptures were created and are scattered throughout the town, some of which are shown above. David Harding went on to found the Department of Environmental Art at the Glasgow School of Art whose alumni include: Douglas Gordon, David Shrigley, Nathan Coley, Christine Borland and Martin Boyce.

References:

Daniel Defoe, (1724), *A Tour Through the Whole Islands of Great Britain*, (New Haven, Yale University Press, 1991 edition), (p.346).

Buildings at Risk Register for Scotland: Leslie House

RCAHMS, Canmore: Leslie House

The Crossroads of Emptiness

absence of presence at the crossroads of emptiness

Now playing: supersilent - *supersilent 6*
Methil, 17th April 2014

A Silent Witness to the Stories of Place

The unfolding spiral begins with the star, the sea and the fishes.

A story of place formed at the threshold of land and tidal flows. Named after the earliest human dwellings, the caves. Inhabited and used for thousands of years by the Picts, early Christians, Norsemen and smugglers, all leaving behind, evidence of that human need to make a mark. Their drawings of fish, serpents, sacred goats, deer and swans incised into stone as silent witness of their stories.

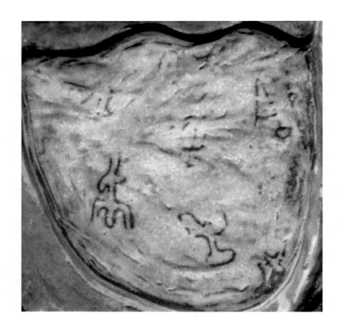

Walking down the aptly named School Wynd in East Wemyss, (the place-name of Wemyss derives from the Gaelic *uamh*, 'cave'), you encounter a colourful piece of public art commemorating the history of the village. From the earliest beginnings of that liminal space between land and sea, there are later references to the nearby ruined castle of MacDuff, linked with the Thane of Fife, slayer of Macbeth. The distinctive red wheels of the Michael Colliery's pithead winding gear represents the more recent industrial, mining heritage.

Like the whorls on a snail's shell, an unfolding of time layered on place.

This place.

A place which holds and retains memory.

Why here, on this small, rough-cast covered, structure?

A small plaque sits to the left on exposed brick work:

IN MEMORY OF
MICHAEL SWINTON BROWN
AGED 15 YEARS
DIED 19th FEBRUARY 1909

We can't learn too much from this. A memorial to a young boy, Michael Swinton Brown who died, aged 15, over 100 years ago.

Knowing what we now know, the cross-hatching on the brick work takes on an eerie significance:

Is this place speaking

of that violent energy

sustained slashing

- criss-cross, criss-cross

The need to make a mark?

≈

On 19th February, 1909, young Michael Brown did what he had to do every Friday. An apprentice clerk for the East Wemyss linen manufacturing firm, G & J Johnston, it was his task to take the tram to nearby Buckhaven to collect the weekly factory wages from the Royal Bank of Scotland. He would return to East Wemyss by tram and walk down School Wynd and back to the factory along the seashore. On this particular day another East Wemyss resident alighted from the tram just behind Michael.

Alexander Edmonstone, aged 23, was an unemployed miner who had moved, with his family, to the village from Edinburgh seven years previously. At exactly 11.54 am, Edmonstone watched Michael Brown set off down School Wynd carrying his brown leather bag containing £85. A few minutes later, Michael Brown entered the brick-built public lavatory and was shortly followed in by Alexander Edmonstone.

It is not exactly clear what happened in the next few minutes as no weapon was ever found but Michael Brown was murdered in a brutal and bloody assault. Edmonstone left with the bag of money and Michael's watch and chain. He followed the course of the Black Burn before ditching the bag and bank pass-book on the seashore near to MacDuff's Castle. Edmonstone knowing that he would be under suspicion, walked 12 miles to Strathmiglo, before catching a train to Perth and then on to Glasgow the following morning. Travelling on to

Paisley, Edmonstone faked a suicide note which he left on the parapet of the bridge over the River Cart:

I murdered Mickey Brown - AE. You will find my body at the foot of the water nearby. I filled my pockets with stones. I bid goodbye to mother. Goodbye - Alexander Edmonstone.

Police dragged the river, obviously without success, and 'Wanted' posters were issued throughout the country offering a reward of £100 leading to an arrest. A month later, Edmonstone had managed to travel to Manchester to take up lodgings under the assumed identity of Alexander Edwards. A fellow lodger had been visiting Whitworth police station to apply for a hawkers licence when he noticed the 'Wanted' poster for Edmonstone and particularly noticed a reference to the watch stolen from Brown. He was sure he had seen this watch and convinced that his fellow lodger was Edmonstone.

Edmonstone was duly arrested and entered a defence of insanity at his trial. However, the jury only took ten minutes to deliver a unanimous verdict of guilty of murder. Edmonstone was hanged at Perth prison on 6th July 1910.

≈

The public lavatory in School Wynd has long since been bricked up. Now it's a site on which the unfolding stories of place have been written.

A place that holds and retains memory.

A silent witness to the stories of place.

≈

Now playing: The Durutti Column - 'Requiem Again' from *Vini Reilly*

12th March 2014

References:

Alexander Edmonstone, 'Court Case 1909, July 8th and 9th', The Fife Post

Molly Whittington-Egan, *The Stockbridge Baby Farmer*, (Castle-Douglas: Neil Wilson Publishing, 2013).

The Wemyss Caves

William Gear - CoBrA artist and Monuments Man from Methil

William Gear - Landscape, (1951)

the landscape of pitheads, the sea, rocks, castles, trees, storms and poverty marked his earliest identity with a place and probably remained the most influential to his art.

he once described his paintings as 'statements of kinship with the natural world'

≈

Amongst a fine display of Scottish Colourists, McTaggarts and Glasgow Boys, a painting hangs in the collection of the newly refurbished Kirkcaldy Galleries titled *Intérieur noir* (1950). It's an abstract expressionist collision of angular black lines and post-war greys, leavened by hints of primary green and red. The painting is by Methil born, William Gear (1915 - 1997) and dates from Gear's 'Cobra Years' when he was one of only two British members of the post-war, European, avant-garde movement CoBrA. Two of the leading instigators of CoBrA, Asger Jorn (1914 - 1973) and

Constant Anton Nieuwenhuys, aka 'Constant' (1920 - 2005) would later become founding members of the Situationist International.

William Gear - Intérieur noir (1950).

≈

Sitting in the dark in the forgetting chamber. The trailer on the cinema screen is for a film called *The Monuments Men*. Directed by and starring George Clooney, the film looks to be a light-hearted comedy romp with a cast featuring Bill Murray, Matt Damon, John Goodman and Cate Blanchett amongst others. The trailer suggests a plot revolving around an unlikely band of allied troops tasked with finding and protecting important works of Art that the Nazis have stolen. At the time, I don't really think a lot about this but it is clear from the preview that this will not be cinéma vérité.

≈

Approach Row, East Wemyss

Rows of miners cottages still stand squat and solid in the village of East Wemyss which sits between Kirkcaldy and Methil. The pithead winding gear of the Michael colliery would once have defined the surrounding landscape. At the time, the Michael was Scotland's largest pit, but with a history of gas build up and spontaneous combustion underground. On 9th September 1967, a disastrous fire broke out in the mine. Although 302 men managed to escape, nine were killed and much of the coal reserves were destroyed. A memorial to the men stands in the village.

On the way to East Wemyss we had stopped at the site of the Frances Colliery, down the road at Dysart. The mine closed in 1989 but the pithead winding gear remains. A towering presence in the landscape evoking something of *The Wicker Man*. An industrial ghost of angular dark lines and winding wheels etched against the muffled blues and greys of a cold, damp, February afternoon.

On a more detailed view, we cannot help but be reminded of Gear's *Intérieur noir:*

This image of the pithead lingers as we imagine tracing the footsteps of William Gear's formative years around the streets and coastal paths of East Wemyss. It doesn't take long before we also encounter the sea, the rocks, the ruined castle, the caves, and the trees.

≈

A painting is not a construction of colours and lines, but an animal, a night, a scream, a human being - or all of these.

Constant

Constant - Animaux (1949)

Corneille - l'homme dans la ville (1952)

Prior to their involvement in the early phase of the Situationist International, Constant and Asger Jorn were key figures in the CoBrA avant-garde group. CoBrA was formed in November 1948 after six disaffected delegates walked out of a conference in Paris discussing proposals for an 'International Centre For The Documentation of Avant-Garde Art'. The dissident group convened at *Café Notre-Dame,* and brought together: Constant, Karel Appel, and Corneille's *Experimentele Groep in Holland;* Christian Dotremont and Joseph Noiret's *Revolutionary Surrealist Group* from Belgium and Asger Jorn's *Høst Group* from Denmark.

Dotremont came up with the name CoBrA (made up from Copenhagen, Brussels, and Amsterdam) and a short founding statement:

the only reason to maintain international activity is experimental and organic collaboration, which avoids sterile theory and dogmatism.

There was no uniform CoBrA style but the artists were united in searching for new paths of creative expression based on spontaneity and experiment and complete freedom of colour and form. They drew their inspiration in particular from children's drawings, primitive art forms and from the work of Paul Klee. Most of the founding artists had experienced life under German occupation and shared similar aspirations following World War II: a new society and a new art. The artists shared an interest in Marxism and saw themselves as a 'red Internationale' that would lead to a new people's art.

CoBrA had a relatively short existence and was dissolved in November 1951. However in this short space of time it distinguished itself from other post-war artist groups by being a manifestly international movement with a number of Cobra artists also collaborating in smaller, loose, cross-border exhibitions.

Britain had only two artists who became part of the CoBrA group. Both were born in Fife. Stephen Gilbert (1910 - 2007) was born in Wormit (1) and William Gear was born in Methil.

William Gear

(Gear) speaks about being inspired by Fifeshire harbours, pit heads, naked trees and hedgerows reminding us that he is essentially a landscape artist whose use of solid, black lines refers to Léger, the Forth Railway Bridge, and medieval stained glass windows (a common reference among Cobra artists).

William Gear - Caged Yellow (1996)

Gear was born in Methil into the hardships of a poor mining family and grew up in the nearby village of East Wemyss. Initially the family lived in a miners row of cottages in Randolph Street and later in Approach Row. His father worked in the local pits, but had creative interests including photography and growing flowers. When young Bill began to show an aptitude for art, he was fully encouraged. Inspiration came from local teachers, the local library and visits to Kirkcaldy Art Gallery to view "Old McTaggart and Peploe." A visit to an Edvard Munch exhibition in Edinburgh also made a huge impression. On finishing school Bill was encouraged to apply for a place at Edinburgh College of Art. Money was an issue for the family however small grants were available from Fife Education Authority, the 'Carnegie' and the Miners Welfare which made this feasible. As Gear recounts:

"this was rather lucky and it was a special Scottish thing or even a Fife thing, because the Fife Education Authority was quite left-wing, even Communist at one time and they very very much encouraged it, the education ... and of course, the Carnegie and the Miners and in one way and the other, I was able to function..."(2).

Gear studied painting at Edinburgh College of Art, 1932–36, where he recounts: "I was already doing my own thing a bit and being hauled over the coals for it, you know being advised to look at Ingres..." A year in Europe, on a travelling scholarship followed, where he ended up in Paris studying with Ferdinand Léger. It is likely that Gear first encountered Asger Jorn at this time as Jorn was working with Léger on his murals for the International Exhibition of 1937.

With the outbreak of the Second World War, Gear was called up to serve in the Royal Signal Corps in Europe and the Middle East. However, he still found time to paint - mostly works on paper of damaged landscapes. He managed to stage exhibitions in Jerusalem, Tel Aviv, and Cairo as well as one-man shows in Siena and Florence.

Monuments Man

When starting to find out a bit more about William Gear, I had no idea that he had in fact been one of the Monuments Men which George Clooney's film supposedly turns into a historic caper. There were around 350 men and women from 13 nations signed up to the Allied Forces' Monuments, Fine Arts and Archives (MFAA) section, during and immediately after the war. During 1946–7, Gear worked for the MFAA and was tasked with securing the safety of the Berlin Art Collection in Schloss Celle. He also organised an important series of modern art exhibitions, including work deemed by the Nazis as 'Degenerate Art' including Picasso and the German Expressionists. In particular, he promoted the work of Karl Otto Gotz who had been banned from exhibiting by the Nazis. Gear became a good friend of Gotz and later introduced him into the CoBrA circle.

Introduction to Cobra

It was during a period of army leave to Paris, in 1947, that Gear was introduced to Constant and Corneille by fellow Fifer, Stephen Gilbert. Gear had already met Jorn before the war and he also knew Jean-Michel

Atlan and Jean Dubuffet. Gear therefore had social connections with the European avant-garde prior to the formation of CoBrA and when he demobbed in 1947, he headed for Paris and soon established a one-room studio at 13 Quai des Grands Augustins. Within a year there were exhibitions at two of the pioneering Paris salons and a first one-man show at the Galerie Arc en Ciel.

Gear was invited by Constant and Jorn to exhibit at CoBrA shows in Amsterdam and Copenhagen in 1949, alongside Corneille and Appel. In the same year, he exhibited alongside Jackson Pollock at Betty Parson's Gallery in New York.

Whilst Gear's paintings could be described as a 'reinvigorated form of abstract expressionism' many display a suggestion of landscape, not least in the recurring titles:

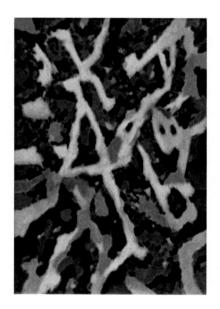 

Spring Song (1951)   Landscape (1950)

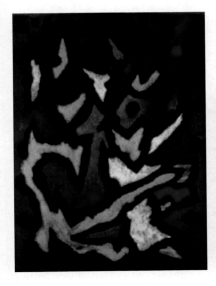

Autumn Landscape (1950)   Landscape (1949)

There was always a link with nature, I never denied nature really. Even in those extreme abstract themes we have been looking at, there is an equivalence to, observable form. I don't say nature in the naturalistic sense but of observable forms. They may be telegraph poles or stakes or trees or structures or, as I am looking out the window now, I mean, I can see, I can see my painting in two or three different ways. There is the severe architectural modern structure over there and at the same time trees and foliage and blossom and light through the tree. I mean, there is my painting you see. This is where it comes from. I don't necessarily sit down and paint that, but I am aware of it.

Festival of Britain 1950

Gear returned to the UK in 1950, recently married to Charlotte Chertok, and with a young son - David - in tow. It was an opportune moment for Gear who, out of sixty artists invited to submit, was one of six artists awarded a Festival of Britain Purchase Prize. Gear's painting was a huge canvas - *Autumn Landscape* - and the only abstract work selected. Illustrating just how little some things change over time, *The Daily Telegraph and Daily Mail* took great exception to this 'waste of public money' and urged readers to complain to their Members of Parliament. The result was the Chancellor of the Exchequer, Hugh Gaitskill, being asked in the House of Commons whether he was satisfied with the expenditure of public money on a painting that had been described as 'trash'. Gaitskill deferred to the decision of the distinguished international jury who had awarded the prizes which represented a broad section of British Art.

William Gear - Autumn Landscape (1951)

Gear makes the point that the whole adverse reaction came from a small 3"x 2" black and white reproduction printed in the *Daily Telegraph* before the exhibition had opened and anyone had actually seen the picture.

Gear became curator of the Towner Gallery in Eastbourne from 1958 to 1964, where he managed to change the local authority's collection policy from Victorian and local views to securing the foundation of a major collection of post-war British art. He became head of the Faculty of Fine Art at Birmingham College of Art in 1964, a post from which he retired in 1975.

Gear continued to paint until the end of his life and whilst out of critical favour for most of the 1960s and 1970s, a renewed interest and retrospective appreciation of the CoBrA movement has gone some way to reverse this. The major *Cobra 1948-51* exhibition in 1982, at the Musee d'Art Moderne, Paris, included works by Gear and Stephen Gilbert and Cobra enthusiast Karel van Stuijvenberg has also been a prominent supporter. A retrospective of Gear's *The Cobra Years* was held at the Redfern Gallery in 1987 and a much larger exhibition *Paintings from the 1950s* in 2006. The Cobra Museum of Modern Art was opened in Amstelveen, near Amsterdam in 1995 with Gear invited to attend the ceremonial opening. Only a few weeks before his death, he was awarded a Leporello Award, appropriately instigated by fellow artists and presented by the Lower Saxony government. This recognised Gear's service in the MFAA and the promotion of "democratic art and artistic freedom." Today, Gears work sits in public collections around the world including collections in the cities and towns of: Kirkcaldy, Aberdeen, Amstelveen, Belfast, Birmingham, Brighton, Buffalo, New York, Canberra, Caracas, Chichester, Cincinnati, Eastbourne, Edinburgh, Fort Lauderdale, Glasgow, Hereford, Kendal, Liege, Lima, London, Manchester, Middlesbrough, Nelson, Newcastle, New York, Ottawa, Oxford, Perth, Rye, Southampton, Stirling, Sydney, Stromness, Tel Aviv, Toledo, Toronto.

William Gear - Les Arbres (1950)

William Gear - Winter Structure (1955-56)

William Gear - Winter Landscape (1949)

≈

We finish our walk around these fundamental landscapes surprised by how much we appear to recognise, see or feel in Gear's work. One final thought occurs as we pass Methil Docks which in Gear's childhood would have been a bustling industrial complex exporting Fife coal around the world. The coal hoist structures for loading the ships may have disappeared but new industrial beasts are presently being constructed.

Perhaps a symbol of transition from a carbon economy towards a more hopeful low-carbon future. We wonder whether these structures will function as the pithead did for Gear. Burning themselves in to the (un)conscious mind of those local artists who will take it, remake it and connect it to the wide wide world. If the local support structures are in place...

Now Playing: Stereolab - Cobra and Phases Group Play Voltage in the Milky Night

20th February 2014

Notes and references:

(1) Perhaps a future post on Stephen Gilbert will follow.

(2) Any quotes attributed to Gear and much of his life background comes from a phenomenal 278 page oral transcription: *National Life Stories, Artists' Lives, William Gear interviewed by Tessa Sidey*. Recorded at various dates during 1995. © The British Library.

Other texts:

William Gear, The Cobra Years 1948-1951, The Redfern Gallery, 1987.

William Gear 1915-1997, Paintings from the 1950s, The Redfern Gallery, 2006.

John McEwen, William Gear (London: Lund Humphries, 2003).

Tessa Sidey, 'Obituary, William Gear' The Independent, Monday 10th March, 1997.

Cobra Museum of Modern Art, Amstelveen.

BBC, Your Paintings, William Gear

All images of the paintings of William Gear used with the kind permission of David Gear

Pterodactyl Attack in the Industrial Edgelands

Now Playing: Mogwai - *The Hawk is Howling*

Methil, 8th February 2014

Once We Looked to the Horizon

Once we looked to the horizon.

How can we see now?

≈

Encased

in the white wall

a pulse, a tracing

an inscription of breath.

An acronym, or

a beginning

an interruption, or

an end?

≈

Wind-blown,

brush strokes.

Impasto smears

- the sky

a feathered script

of light

≈

At the ghost pier

the ebb and flow

of memory

and forgetting

≈

Weather soaked

histories

etched - in wood

a redundancy of nails

≈

A polished pewter sky

dreams a wash of

copper-burnished kisses

≈

an invitation,

the pull towards

the edge

to sit and stare.

Listening

to the lichens

singing

≈

On the cliff top,

who is watching

the solitary watcher?

≈

and at the bench

an outward gaze

to remember

and once again

look beyond

the edge of the horizon.

≈

Musings from a short walk in the village of Aberdour, Fife, on 28th December 2013.

Thanks to @emmaZbolland for "Pewter light" in response to an earlier tweet of the Ghost Pier.

Now playing: *Translucence* - John Foxx and Harold Budd.
9th January, 2014

Encounter with Waving, Smiling Robot

Aberdour, Fife.

Now playing: Simply Saucer - *Here Come the Cyborgs*
28th December 2013

Rosyth Edgelands Dérive

 We are in dangerous territory, walking westward out of the town of Rosyth, along the A985, one of 'Britain's killer roads'. This arterial incision into the connective tissue of the Rosyth edgelands is to fully engage with the disruptive polarities emanating from two monolithic structures, which have recently appeared on either side of the road. There is a real sense that the landscape, skyscape and mindscape have all been irretrievably altered. Whether this is benign or malevolent who can say? It is this that we must investigate and address head-on with our *dérive*. Establish relations, resist, remap, and reclaim as necessary.

As we set off, along the ridgeline of the A985, there is an undercurrent of fear that a vortex of radiant, colliding energies may threaten to rip us, stalking walkers, apart or even lure us into the path of oncoming traffic on the killer road. This is a risk that we are prepared for and must take.

≈

The first stretch of road between two roundabouts is almost classic edgeland topography. On the right hand side, the small *favela* of allotments, with waves of canes, poles, pallet fencing and water butts; shanty sheds and corrugated iron knitted together with plastic pipework. There is a disordered/orderliness about the place; a charivari of utility and resourceful exchange, which resists the carefully manicured garden porn displayed in garden centres and lifestyle magazines. You can tell that this is land that is worked, loved and loves back.

On the other side of the road, past the football pitch, stands the 'old Lexmark building', supposedly the location of 'the factory' in Gregory Burke's play *Gagarin Way*. We have investigated this building before and continue to monitor its energy levels, but no sign of the smoked salmon fishes as yet.

As we traverse over the second roundabout, there are clear intimations that the interzone between the town and edgelands has been breached. For the car driver, flooring it off the roundabout and opening up to the straight road ahead it's as if the gravitational pull of the town loses its grip, supplanted by a carnivalesque impulse to wind down the window and toss the debris of consumer society into the hedgecomb of trees and shrubs edging the road. Here lies a graveyard of inert excess, an inventory of impulse purchases; eating and drinking on the hoof and a veritable time capsule of the non-biodegradable floatsam of consumer culture. Like true twitchers, we must record our spoils:

Diet Coke, Fosters, Tennant's, McCoys, Irn Bru, Sprite, Muller, McDonalds, Pepsi, Corona, Red Rooster, Lucozade, KP, Dr Pepper, Costa, Coke, Yorkie, Milky Bar, Pampers, Cadbury's Buttons, Starbucks, Walkers, Carling, Graham's Dairies, Tesco, Diet Pepsi, Asda, Smoking Kills, Ginsters, Pizza Hut, Golden Wonder, Red Bull, Powerade, Wild Bean Cafe, Huggies, Greggs, Snickers...

Fired up on caffeine,

the sugar rush floods

the synapses,

foot to the floor,

screech, toss

and off.

We are also struck by how the edgelands are places where things are simply forgotten about. Advertising signs from a more benign economic environment offering 'Industrial Units for Sale or Lease' are falling down and are never replaced; road signs tilt at 45 degrees; posters on substations intimate long forgotten concerts and doors on the mysterious roadside bunkers have all disappeared.

We are now out in the true edgelands, hugging the ribbon of verge by the side of the road as every vehicle utterly tanks it past us. We are pebbledashed by huge swathes of road spray and the draught, from the huge artic lorries that pass, threatens to pull us foot-powered perambulators into the middle of road. However, the objects of our effort and attention can now be clearly seen on either side of the road. We can feel their energies drilling into us and can only marvel at the scale of their transforming presence on this stretch of the edgelands. As long as we can stay vigilant and remain on the ribbon verge, we can resist the siren call urging us into the *killer road*.

Over to the right, in the middle distance, is a 100 metre column, on top of which sits a rotating turbine with three, colossal, scythe -like blades. This somehow reminds us of the free gifts of plastic spinners that you used to get sellotaped to the front cover of children's comics like *The Beano* and *The Dandy*. Thus we have a *name* for our monster - *Spinner* - a vital part of the engagement and neutralisation process. Spinner is of such a scale that it doesn't look quite real. It's as if it is projecting some perspective morphing force field which shrinks or obliterates the elements within the landscape which offer any indication of human scale.

Spinner belongs to FMC Technologies, a Houston, Texas headquartered business, which manufactures subsea systems for the oil and gas and renewables industry. The 1.5MW turbine is projected to supply up to 40% of the energy needs at their Dunfermline facility and was financed by Triodos, the ethical bank. We stand and watch the strange poetry of the rotating blades dancing with the wind, quite hypnotic and completely silent from our vantage point. There is some sense of good energy radiating from this structure and there is a fluidity and engagement with the elements. Spinner could probably only be a product of the edgelands. A place where a turbine of this size can be erected then lost and forgotten, despite its landscape transforming qualities.

If Spinner has a slightly ethereal, alchemical quality, transforming wind into electricity, over to our left is a structure that looks as if it is marauding up towards the ridge, like a mechanised robotic toy about to attack. This is the aptly named Goliath crane recently transported from China's Shanghai Zhenhua Port Machinery Co Ltd, where it was manufactured. Goliath is the largest crane installed in the UK and across its 120m beam is the clearly visible signage:

aircraft carrier alliance

Goliath sits in Rosyth Dockyard which lies over the hill down on the Forth. In effect, we are only seeing the top of the crane which at 90m high

almost rivals Spinner in height. Goliath is part of the most expensive project in British naval history with two aircraft carriers presently being constructed at £3 billion a pop. We have already been told that once constructed, one will be mothballed immediately and the other will have no planes to fly from it. Try explaining this logic to a five year old. The carriers are to be named HMS Queen Elizabeth and HMS Prince of Wales. The sheer folly, financial carnage and symbolism of this whole escapade is such that it almost fries our collective brain into meltdown. However, very soon we are all whistling and singing Elvis Costello's *Shipbuilding* - the Robert Wyatt version naturally - so we can hum the piano solo with our kazoos. This has the desired effect, tames the beast and calm descends. As we walk further along the road, we can gain a better vantage point to look down over the dockyard and see the true scale of Goliath. Our fear turns to pity as we realise that all we are looking at is simply a dumb, beast of burden, a heavy lifter, on which has been foisted the indignity of jingoistic colours, the White Ensign flag and the reek of failed empire. Also lurking down there, somewhere in the bowels are seven decommissioned nuclear submarines, still radioactive and we are reminded of some possibly apocryphal tales of technician's metal-capped boots glowing green in the dark. Isn't it amazing what can be buried in the edgelands.

Back on the A985 and another juggernaut threatens to drag us into the road as we alight on Windylaw Path which leads down to the villages of Limekilns and Charlestown. We've had enough of the road but happy to have got the measure of Spinner and Goliath. Our dérive receptors are once again activated when we read that Windylaw Path is a coffin road.

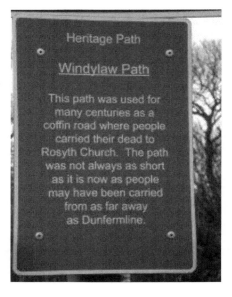

Who could resist that and was Limekilns not mentioned in Stevenson's *Kidnapped?*

As we head up the coffin road, a buzzard soars overhead...

Now playing: Brian Lavelle – *Lambent*

9th March 2012

On the Coffin Road

We approach the village from the North by the coffin road known as Windylaw. A sign indicates that this path was used for many centuries by people to carry their dead to Rosyth Church. Sometimes they would come from as far away as Dunfermline.

...

The ground is sodden underfoot and standing still you can feel the ticklish trickle of rivulets, running around your boots off the slight incline. This is the first day of reasonable weather for weeks and it feels good to stand under the mottled blue canopy and listen to the murmur of the flowing field.

L

i

s

t

e

n

Windylaw meanders up towards a small copse of trees. We are greeted by the guardian of the forest, a snuffling, wood-hedgehog type apparition which looks like it could have come straight out of *Pogles Wood*.

A woodpecker industriously loops its rrrrrat-a-tat-tat rhythm but remains unseen. We stand still and stare but there is no dart of kinetic red against gray bark. Instead, one particular tree conjures up a Medusa like quality. The branches appear to move, twisting and writhing like a cauldron of snakes.

Windylaw meanders through the trees and we walk alongside all of the ghosts who have trampled this path over many centuries.

How many stopped to make their mark such as Toad has done here?

Once over the ridge of hill, we start to descend towards the shoreline and the village of Limekilns which we can see off to the right. We leave the path briefly to take in the vista over the Forth Estuary.

In many ways a picturesque enough view. Over the farmer's fields to the river Forth and beyond to West Lothian. However, no view is ever as 'innocent' as it seems so let us tilt our heads a little bit further to the left and to the right. Let us ponder on what we can see...

...

Firstly off to the left, lies Rosyth Dockyard:

The picture is not great but you can clearly see *Goliath's* looming presence of whom we have written before:

"Goliath is the largest crane installed in the UK and part of the most expensive project in British naval history with two aircraft carriers presently being constructed at £3 billion a pop. We have already been told that once constructed, one will be mothballed immediately and the other will have no planes to fly from it. Try explaining this logic to a five year old. The carriers are to be named HMS Queen Elizabeth and HMS Prince of Wales. The sheer folly, financial carnage and symbolism of this whole escapade is such that it almost fries our collective brain into meltdown. However, very soon we are all whistling and singing Elvis Costello's Shipbuilding – the Robert Wyatt version naturally – so we can hum the piano solo with our kazoos. This has the desired effect, tames the beast and calm descends. As we walk further along the road, we can gain a better vantage point to look down over the dockyard and see the true scale of Goliath. Our fear turns to pity as we realise that all we are looking at is simply a dumb, beast of burden, a heavy lifter, on which has been foisted the indignity of jingoistic colours, the White Ensign flag and the reek of failed empire. Also lurking down there, somewhere in the bowels are seven decommissioned nuclear submarines, still radioactive and we are reminded of some possibly apocryphal tales of technicians metal-capped boots glowing green in the dark. Isn't it amazing what can be buried in the edgelands."

On the same day as our walk (31st March 2013), a number of articles appear in the press to indicate that Rosyth Dockyard has been chosen for a pilot project to break up some of the nuclear submarines, prompting fears it could become a dumping ground for radioactive waste. (Ignoring the somewhat obvious fact that it already is). The one fairly fundamental snag in this proposal is that no site or facility has yet been identified to store radioactive material safely. (It is going to be there for a long, long time). I suspect that our inventory of Empire and hubristic bravado - HMS Dreadnought, HMS Churchill, HMS Resolution, HMS Repulse, HMS Renown, HMS Revenge and HMS Swiftsure may continue to sit and rust for many years to come, hopefully with the nuclear reactors remaining intact.

You can also just make out the Forth Bridges, beyond the dockyard, in the above photographs. The iconic red diamonds of the Victorian rail bridge and the twin suspension towers of the not inelegant road bridge. Both, arguably, engineering 'works of art'. Construction work is now well underway for a third bridge to join them. It would appear that the existing road bridge has literally become a piece of auto-destructive art. Road vehicle usage, far in excess of what was originally envisaged has reduced the life of the suspension cables and consequently the bridge. (Although there is some debate about this). The result will be a new road bridge with an increased capacity to continue to satiate our desire for car travel. Build it and it will be filled is the usual outcome of transport policy so perhaps we stand as witnesses to the birth of yet another engineering marvel sown with the seeds of its eventual auto-destruction.

As is becoming evident, the Forth is still very much a working river and from our viewpoint it would not be unusual to see a container ship - the new packhorse of global capitalism - chugging up the central channel to Grangemouth container port to drop off its wares. Alternatively, it could be a British warship off for some 'munitions and maintenance support' at Crombie Pier which is part of the sealed off Crombie Munitions Depot.

This is very close to Crombie Point where Jules Verne and Aristide Hignard disembarked from an Edinburgh steamer in 1859 to continue their travels through Fife and Scotland. This journey inspired Verne's novel *The Green Ray*.

'Le Rayon Vert'

And beyond Crombie Pier lies the Grangemouth petrochemical plant, Scotland's only oil refinery. An industrial city of chimneys and cooling towers, belching steam, and when darkness falls, shooting dramatic flares into the sky against a wash of sodium hue.

Chances are that all the cars sitting nose to tail on the Forth Bridges will ultimately get their petrol from here. Just another nodal point in the network of global petrochem dollars.

OK surely that's it. But no. Strain your eyes to the far right and another iconic sight can be zoomed into view. The chimney of the coal powered Longannet Power Station. I'm sure it keeps our lights on but is regularly towards the top of the charts in any survey of 'most polluting power stations' in the UK and Europe.

Longannet Power Station – Zoom

Anyway this digression is just an illustration of how a landscape view is never neutral. On one level, yes this is a beautiful landscape. However, this is also a landscape inextricably linked into the ebb and flow of the global capitalist economy, or on a more pessimistic note, is there any more perfect spot to catalogue and observe the agents and consequences of what George Monbiot calls the Age of Entropy. (Thanks to Liminal City for alerting us to this). At the very least, the psychogeographer can reverse the panoptical gaze of the modern political machine. Standing here *we* can use landscape as a mirror to reflect back. We can see the war machines, the entropic processors of fossil fuels, how the local is connected to the global. On this spot we can be the watchers. We can see what you are up to and imagine and enact alternative possibilities. (Such as going for a walk!).

...

We continue our descent down Windylaw which edges the perimeter of the newer built part of Limekilns. A desire path breaks off to the left and we soon find ourselves at the rear of the old ruined Rosyth Church. Records indicate that the church dates back to the 12th century when it is mentioned in the charter sent to the monks of Inchcolm Abbey in 1123. The church ceased to be used as a place of worship sometime between 1630 and 1648. You can clearly appreciate why the coffin

road evolved. Even today, the only access to this spot is by walking or possibly by boat. Whilst doing a bit of research, a curious entry in the RCHMS archive records catches the eye. In 1998 a "stray human mandible was found on a grassy area just south of Rosyth Old Kirk burial ground by Mr Walmsley of Inverkeithing. The very weathered and friable bone belonged to a child aged 6-9 years."

there is none more lonely and eerie than Rosyth, at anyrate at the close of a winter day, when a rising wind is soughing through the bare branches, and the sea is beginning to moan and tramp to and fro over rock and shingle.

John Geddie, *The Fringes of Fife*, (1894)

Unlike Geddie, we find the church reflecting sunlight on a bright, still morning with just the slightest intimation of Spring in the air. Little of the original structure remains. Only the East gable and part of the North wall. A mort house still stands, built at a later date, to no-doubt frustrate the profitable enterprise of the resurrectionists (body snatchers) who are known to have prowled the coastal graveyards, often arriving by boat.

East Gable –Outer

The churchyard, as in all churchyards, is full of stories. Manicured fragments of past lives lived. How much of a person can be captured when reduced to a few lines of inscription on a gravestone? In many cases, the weather and the passage of time work to gradually efface even this small act of material remembrance. Chiselled stone is returned to smoothness as the distant past becomes literally more difficult to read yielding up only broken fragments and guesses.

Fractured

Fragments & Guesses

Tombs are Trifles

Lost at Sea

This gravestone below is particularly rich in symbolism: the trumpet blowing Angel of the Resurrection; the *memento mori* skull as a representation of death and the hourglass denoting the passing of time.

Angel of Resurrection, skull & hourglass

This stone was erected in the year of the French Revolution:

1789

We were really intrigued with this one. The reversed numeral "7" in particular. Also the fact that four sets of initials are on the gravestone?

Nowadays, the quiet graveyard appears to be a haven for bird life. During our visit, blackbirds scurried amongst the leaves whilst a robin dotted around the gravestones following us.

One last photo before we leave and it's only later that we notice the ghostly halo around the door frame. Saturated light I'm sure but who knows?

On leaving the the graveyard, we head right which leads to a pleasant shoreline walk along to Limekilns. Looking over the water there is even a hint of Glastonbury Tor over in West Lothian. It's the tower folly of The House of the Binns, Tam Dalyell's family home.

It's a short walk to Limekilns and as we approach we are reminded of David Balfour and Alan Breck who visit the village in Robert Louis Stevenson's *Kidnapped*:

"about ten in the morning, mighty hungry and tired, came to the little clachan of Limekilns. This is a place that sits near in by the water-side, and looks across the Hope to the town of the Queensferry."

(*Kidnapped*, Chapter XXVI, End of the Flight: We Pass the Forth).

We will write-up what we found in Limekilns and Charlestown another day.

Now Playing: Current 93 - *Baalstorm, Sing Omega*

4th April 2013

References:

Alan Reid, Limekilns and Charlestown: A Historical Sketch and Descriptive Sketch of a Notable Fifeshire Neuk, (Dunfermline: A. Romanes, 1903).

The Poppies are in the Field

The poppies are in the field

But don't ask me what that means

- Julian Cope

There is no
long march of progress
in this field.
No future
enlightenment
to strive for.
                    Only
this eternal play
of returning.
A cycle of flowering flame
                smouldering
                            to ash
in the rooted earth
underneath my feet.

That we find a crystal or a poppy beautiful means that we are less alone, that we are more deeply inserted into existence than the course of a single life would lead us to believe.

John Berger - *The White Bird*

Homer mentions poppies in the *Iliad*, comparing the head of a dying warrior to that of a hanging poppy flower.

The god Morpheus made crowns out of the poppy flowers and gave them to those he wanted to put to sleep. Poppy flowers were used to decorate the temple.

The Greeks have a legend that explains how the poppy came to be called the Corn Poppy. The poppy was created by the god of sleep, Somnus. Ceres, the goddess of grain, was having difficulty falling asleep. She was exhausted from searching for her lost daughter; still she couldn't fall asleep and had no energy to help the corn grow. Somnus cooked up a concoction and got her to take it and soon she was sleeping. Rested and relaxed Ceres could then turn her attention to the corn which began to grow. Ever since that time the people believed that poppies growing around cornfields ensure a bountiful harvest. And so was born the Corn Rose, or as we call it today the Corn Poppy.

Adapted from *The Modern Herbal*

But the Poppy is painted glass; it never glows so brightly as when the sun shines through it. Wherever it is seen-against the light or with the light - always, it is a flame, and warms the wind like a blown ruby.

John Ruskin - Proserpina

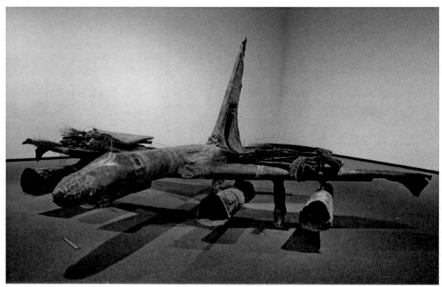

Photo credit: cliff1066™ / Foter.com / CC BY

Angel of History: Poppy and Memory by Anselm Kiefer.

A warplane fabricated of lead

wings laden with books of beaten lead sheets

stuffed with dried poppies.

Photographs taken near Pattiesmuir on 26th June 2013.

Now Playing: Siouxsie and the Banshees - *Poppy Day* & The Teardrop Explodes - *Poppies in the Field*.

Two Spectral Trees - Somewhere North of Devilla Forest

Looking up to the ridge, over the evergreen crowns, two spectral trees hang mid-air in the limpid heat. A smoke spiral, all coiled movement, settles to stillness as a Rorschach blot of charcoal smudge bleeds into sun saturated blue. The universe melts into my hands. A sublime stasis cupped and held close.

For how long is not the right question - linear time is of no help to us here.

The "caw caw" of a black craw - pierces the membrane of this no-time. The moment trickles away, dissolves on the ground, scattering the seeds of its eternal recurrence as memory...

Memory is not an instrument for exploring the past but its theatre. It is the medium of past experience, as the ground is the medium in which dead cities lie interred.

Walter Benjamin

Just a brief extract from what will eventually develop into a longer piece or a series of shorter pieces. We have made a couple of visits to Devilla Forest, near Kincardine, recently and it is clear that it will take us a good few more trips to really get the measure of this place. Our foray into the heart of the forest last week was an exercise in getting hopelessly lost which coupled with the first intimation of Spring was no bad result. The overhead sky, was a cloudless colour field of bleached blue and once the sun was up it felt like the last of the winter murk was being cleansed away. We eventually ended up North of the forest climbing up to a ridge above the tree tops. Here we found the spectral trees and a curious weather mast amongst crumbling drystane dykes.

Devilla Forest is located just North East of Kincardine and the name is said to come from the Gaelic "dubh" and "eilean" meaning "black island". The forest is now run as a commercial tree plantation by the Forestry Commission and consists mainly of Scots Pine, Norway Spruce and Larch. However, the area has a long history of land use with Prehistoric coffins, stone circles and Roman urns all found in different parts of the forest.

There are also plague graves, a stone which a local legend says is marked by the grooves from a witch's apron string and the remains of a World War II explosives research establishment within the forest area. Combine all of that with four lochs/ponds, burns, meadowland and rich wildlife - including red squirrels - and it's easy to see why this site should be worthy of further investigation.

Oh and there is also a history of Big Black Cat sightings. We may have the chance to record one ourselves in The Nature Report Book.

Unfortunately there were no maps:

"I hunt among stones" - Charles Olson.

We had made one previous brief visit to the forest on 23rd February. This date coincided with *Terminalia*, the ancient Roman Festival in honour of the god Terminus who presided over boundaries. Often his statue was merely a post or stone stuck in the ground to mark the boundaries between areas of land. Aware that some psychogeographers throughout the country were commemorating *Terminalia* in some fashion, it was perhaps a serendipitous discovery to find some wonderful local examples in the forest:

This is a Meith Stone which has the St Andrews Cross carved in the top. The stones were used to mark land boundaries and sometimes initials were inscribed on each side of the stone denoting land ownership. Apparently five stones have been found along what would have been the old drove road between Kincardine and Culross.

This enigmatic looking stone is known locally as The Standard Stone, which according to local legend marks the spot where a Danish Army defeated Duncan and his generals Macbeth and Banquo in The Battle of Bordie Moor. (1038). The stone could also have been where the Scots army placed their battle standards, but is more likely to be the base of a medieval stone cross on a parish boundary or a wooden gallows.

From our initial couple of visits, we can *feel* that Devilla is going to yield up some interesting discoveries if we can manage to avoid getting lost next time. Then again that may be no bad thing.

The Owl is awaiting our return.

Now Playing: Boards of Canada - 'You Could Feel the Sky' from *Geogaddi*.

6th March 2013

Cup and Ring - Haunted by a Symbol

I am being haunted by a symbol!

During the summer a visitation to one of the richest sites of ancient psychogeographic energy - Kilmartin Glen.

In particular the cup and ring marks at Auchnabreck, led to a fascination with this symbol that transcends cultures and geographies and yet refuses to yield up any verifiable meaning. Theories abound: possibly aesthetic, ceremonial, territorial or route markers are common propositions.

I stare at my iPod and the podcasting symbol. Whilst ostensibly a human form/antenna enveloped in concentric circles, it is clearly identifiable as a cup and ring symbol.

The latest edition of the marvellous music magazine *The Wire* pops through the letterbox. Cup and ring imagery radiates from the cover.

'Noise in the ether: explorations in the art of radio transmission'. Dialled in, tuned in, picking up the signal.

Last night, N & R are watching The X Factor. Before each contestant performs, they are enveloped in cup and ring digital effects. Channelling their karaoke talents into the receptive cerebrum of popular culture.

In all of these images, I like the idea of transmission; of energy radiating outwards, of ripples on the surface of consciousness being picked up by the tuned in antenna. Perhaps our ancient forebears were also receptive to this idea, long before the discovery of radio waves begat such an adaptable and iconic image. These ancient rock carvings continue to transmit their own seductive energy and whilst the signal to noise ratio is weak, the dials are picking up the broadcast. Even the popular culture charms of the X Factor are not immune.

And what of these ancient symbols within the Fife landscape? I was delighted to find out about some perfectly preserved examples on The Binn (Hill) at Burntisland. A field trip for the Collective beckons.

Now playing: Kayo Dot - *Choirs of the Eye*

10th October 2010

Cup and Ring on The Binn – Burntisland

In a previous post, I wrote of being haunted by the cup and ring symbol. In this wired, digital world, these cross-cultural, cross-geographic ciphers are all around us. Infiltrating our consciousness and yet remaining elusive and enigmatic. Tune in and they will reveal themselves in many unexpected places - from iPods to the X Factor, to packets of washing up powder.

How exciting to discover that some well-preserved marks exist on the north side of The Binn (Hill), the volcanic plug that overlooks Burntisland. It's unlikely that you would stumble across them without having been tipped a nod as to where they are - they have protected themselves well for over 4000 years.

Let's just say that when you find them, the setting makes perfect sense. Vistas out over the Forth, high ground but sheltered. The heavens and stars open above. A place to capture energies of earth, wood, wind and sun; a place to inscribe these enigmas upon stone. Make a mark. An image of transmission; of energy radiating outwards, of ripples on the surface of consciousness being picked up by the tuned in antenna. Perhaps our ancient forebears were also receptive to this idea, way before the discovery of radio waves begat such an adaptable and iconic image.

It's a pleasant walk to the stones. Up through a sheltered path, heady aromas of rain drenched wood bark, soft underfoot. Off to the left the sound of falling water. At the end of the path a steep scramble and over the stile. A pause for breath and across the butterfly strewn meadow, until you pick up the path that heads up to the summit of the Binn. A couple of ducks, glide aimlessly amongst the reeds in the pond on the left. Dragonflies hover like winged shards of stained glass and suddenly they are gone as if dissolved in sunlight. As you commence the climb up the Binn, the rocks are up on the right hand side. A scramble over some rough ground and fallen trees and once you are in the vicinity, you will feel the pull of the rocks and there they are.

There are two key marks. One is a fully complete cup and ring, perfectly preserved. Another smaller one has been started but remains unfinished. I wonder why? It's a blast to close your eyes and think that around 4,000 years ago someone had taken the time - many many hours - to carve these marks into this rock. This rock here - now! We can still only guess why and perhaps it is better that way. Do we want to know that it may have only been for some dull utilitarian purpose? No! It remains here today, something quite beautiful and powerful - expressive human poetry - materially tangible but elusive. If we try to wring out its mysteries with theories and guesswork, meaning slips away, like grains of sand through the fingers.

Carrying on up to the summit of the Binn. There is a 'top of the world' sensation. Burntisland lies, directly below. Once home to Mary Somerville, pioneering mathematician and astronomer and the Reverend Thomas Chalmers, radical, social reformer and founder of the Free Church of Scotland. Once described by Patrick Geddes as 'an anarchist economist beside whom Kropotkin and Reclus are mere amateurs'.

Glinters of sunlight on the Forth to East and West as the wind whips up a frenzy of pebbledash rain. We are forced to take cover in a small natural alcove on the hillside. Sheltering from the elements, thinking of pioneering radicals just as our stone carving friends would have done 4,000 years ago.

Now playing - Franca Sacchi: *En*

4th August 2011

Three Steps ...

≈

Three steps may be all it takes to alter our perception of place

≈

A fairly idyllic view taken last weekend from the Fife Coastal Path at Dalgety Bay. An expansive sky animated by great dollops of scudding cloud, mirrored in the calm, glassy sea. Inchcolm Island lies straight ahead and over to the right, the contours of Edinburgh and Arthur's Seat ink the horizon.

Waders and gulls amble and preen on the bay foreshore with divers, ducks and the occasional seal bobbing in the deeper water.

≈

take three steps back

o

n

e

≈

t

w

o

≈

t

h

r

e

e

≈

...

You find out that you are actually standing on radioactive contaminated land.

The contamination is believed to originate from the residue of radium coated instrument panels that were used in military aircraft. Between 1946 and 1959, over 800 planes were incinerated and the ash was land-filled in the area.

Radioactive material was first detected on a part of the foreshore in 1990 and, since then, more than 1000 radioactive items have been removed.

It has taken twenty-three years for the MoD to be 'officially' named as polluter of the site by the Scottish Environment Protection Agency (SEPA). However, the MoD continue to prevaricate in actually admitting responsibility and most importantly undertaking remediation options. This week, the can has been kicked forward, once again, until September when another 'discussion' between SEPA and the MoD will take place.

There is a possibility that SEPA will be required to formally designate the beach at Dalgety Bay as a radiation-contaminated area. If this happens, it will be the first such designated site in the UK.

"It would be extraordinary that in a Britain that has nuclear storage sites, nuclear processing sites, nuclear weapons and nuclear waste, the beautiful beach at Dalgety Bay would stand out as the first and only radiation-contaminated site in the country."

(Gordon Brown, MP, *Hansard*, 9th July 2013)

The layered traces of human activity embedded in the land takes on another dimension when the presence of absence can be measured in half-lives.

Now playing: Sun Ra - *Nuclear War.*

14th August 2013

The Lundin Links Stones

JULIAN COPE & DONALD ROSS SKINNER

On the cover of Julian Cope's album *Rite* is a picture of three colossal megaliths. The human form giving some indication of the size and scale of this unusual grouping.

Whether a function of crafted intent or the ageing process, the three distinctly shaped stones (especially the foregrounded 'pin head' or finger?) conjure up a strong sense of the uncanny when you see them up close. Imagine my delight when I found out that these beauties, the remains of the largest of all the Scottish four-poster stone circles, are located in Lundin Links. Even more surreal is to find out they are presently located on the second fairway of a ladies golf course.

It was a mild, drizzly day as I snaked along the A915, into the East Neuk. It was a bit of an opportunistic visit so hadn't fully determined the exact location of the stones. All I knew was that they were located on a golf course in Lundin Links. Of course I hadn't realised that there are two golf course in Lundin Links so initially stopped off at The Lundin Golf Club, which has the appearance of catering for the affluent, Edinburgh-on-sea weekenders who tend to congregate around this part of the coast at their weekend cottages. By this time it was a pretty dreich day so not a lot of people were around to ask. I just set off, going on the basis that the size of these monsters should make them fairly easy to track down. However, the landscape didn't feel 'right'. Largo Law was too far away, and the Lundin Club is right on the coast. Nonetheless I had an enjoyable saunter along the seaward side of the links, back towards Leven, watching the white breakers fizz on the shore. I soon realised that this was not a landscape where sacred stones would be erected. It was too windswept, open, and there was no relationship to Largo Law. Back I trudged, gazing up the coast and feeling the wind, spray and drizzle on my face. I had to be guided by the Law - what Julian Cope refers to (rather poetically) as a mother mountain - and set off once again in search of the stones. I soon found some signposts to the Lundin Ladies Golf Club and I could tell that this location was going to yield a more fruitful expedition. I subsequently found out that Lundin Ladies is the oldest ladies golf club in the world (established in 1890) and is run completely independently by the lady members. In the unreconstructed chauvinism of the typical male golf club, there was something quite radical and subversive about all this. It was further confirmed when I asked two ladies who were loading their clubs into the car where I may find the stones and whether I need to seek formal permission to go and have a look. They couldn't have been more welcoming, and it was pleasant to observe their local accents and nay a set of pearls in sight. As indicated, I crunched along the stone path to the starters hut and as soon as you turn the corner, you can see the stones way up the fairway in the distance. Once again, the starter was very welcoming and told me that there was no-one on the course so I could go and have a good look without worrying about any balls passing nearby.

This time the land did 'feel right'. A clear relationship is evident with Largo Law, and the stones nestle in the rolling foothills. Notwithstanding the sand bunkers, tee boxes, and suburban sprawl on the south side, this still feels like a special place, and the light drizzle, absence of people and eerie quietness added to this. As I walked up the edge of the fairway, the sheer size of the stones soon becomes apparent. These are towering monsters at thirteen, seventeen and eighteen feet high, with the finger/pinhead stone, twisting and pointing to the heavens, radiating a strange, seductive energy. There used to be four stones, and apparently the fourth stone lay prostrate until around 1792 before it was no doubt removed for more utilitarian purposes.

There is a local story that Michael Scot, the Wizard of Balwearie, summoned the demon familiars, Prig, Prim and Pricker to the sacred hill of Largo Law with a view to dismantling it. As they began to dig, Scott had a change of plan and their single shovelful was thrown to create the nearby cairn of Norrie's Law at the wonderfully named farm of Baldastard. There is also a local story that a rich goldmine exists somewhere underneath Largo Law and that sheep have returned from grazing on the foothills with golden fleeces.

I guess that these stones must be one of the best kept secrets in Fife, (Scotland?) and yet as a site for experiencing the uncanny, difficult to surpass. I can understand that the good ladies of Lundin Links do not want hordes of trampling visitors all over their gold course, so perhaps there is something poetic that they remain available to the seeker and yet are well looked after and protected by the Lundin Ladies, drawing energy from their mother mountain. I wonder if it helps their golf?

Thanks to Julian Cope's magisterial *The Modern Antiquarian*.

Now playing: *John Barleycorn Reborn: Dark Britannica*, V/A.

12th September 2010

We Walked Side by Side

From the shadows in the twilight

a glint of iridescence.

We walked side by side

through a car park today.

Now Playing: Eivind Aarset - *Dream Logic*

The Wilderness Does Exist - A Field Trip

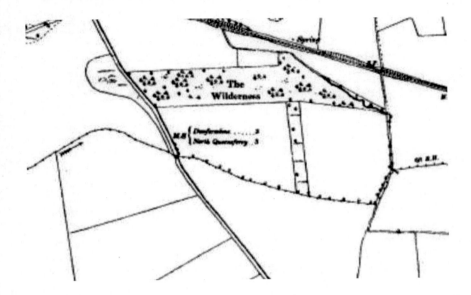

How could we not be intrigued?

Casting an eye over some local maps from the late 1800s. Stumble and trip.

The Wilderness.

An actual place on the map.

The delineated form resembles a long-front-legged cartoon fox. We resist the urge to draw on ears, eyes, nose and a brush. Somewhat ironically, The Wilderness is represented by dotted clumps of trees contrasting with the surrounding patchwork of largely undefined white space.

A field trip beckons. Is it possible to visit The Wilderness as an actual place, rather than just as an idea? Is The Wilderness always just an idea, conjuring up clichéd images of distant rain forests, shifting desert sands or a featureless frozen tundra pulled towards a distant white edge of land and sky. What would *this* Wilderness look like in 2012?

On a sunny December Sunday of 2012 we set off to see what we can find and mentally attempt to visualise the area of the cartoon fox, as it is today. Our best guess is that if anything is left it may now be in the middle of a housing estate in Rosyth, Fife. There could also be a Tesco store and pub planted firmly in its hind quarters...

The above map dates from 1896 which predates the building of Rosyth, Scotland's only Garden City. The town was built to service the Royal Naval Dockyard which began construction in 1909. The original houses were first occupied in 1915 and still stand, exuding a solidity and displaying attractive design features that would be alien to the mass, wooden boxbuilders of today. (Who would bet against the big bad wolf confronting a timber-framed flat pack?). The original tree-lined street plan also remains largely intact although you will have to search harder to find a front garden. Many are now paved over into parking spaces for the ubiquitous car.

Arriving in Rosyth, we orientate ourselves from the railway station and set off. As suspected, it is clear that the rear end of our fox, on the 1896 map, now houses a Tesco store with Cleos pub alongside. The main road through the town - Queensferry Road - dissects a later phase of house building on the other side. As we walk down Queensferry Road, there is certainly no obvious sign or hint of any wilderness. We can see some mature trees lining the side of the road but it is difficult to say whether these could be original Wilderness trees or part of the town landscaping plan. Following our noses we turn left into Wemyss Street and ponder on the name. "Wemyss" is derived from the Gaelic word 'uaimh', meaning 'cave'. There are strong landscape resonances in Fife to the Wemyss caves up the coast, beyond Dysart but we guess that the linkage is more likely to be associated with the landowning Wemyss family. Descended from the MacDuff Earls of Fife, (Macbeth!) the Wemyss built their castle between what is now known as East and West Wemyss. There are certainly no obvious caves around, that we can see, but in appellation terms, the connotation of landed gentry hobnobbing with royalty sits well with the nearby Kings Road and Queensferry Road.

Walking along Wemyss Street, it does occur to us that this may be a short trip. We are surrounded by residential houses and yet looking at the map we must be walking over part of the fox's torso mapped as The Wilderness in 1896. Maybe this is actually a walk of mourning. A wake for an idea that, for whatever reason, resulted in an area of land being named The Wilderness. We can also extrapolate from the local to the global and the sense of the Earth's Wilderness footprint being appropriated, exploited, diminished and perhaps lost forever.

Wemyss Street, Rosyth

We continue to follow the sweep of Wemyss Street and start heading south when we come across a little cul-de-sac named The Woodlands. This feels better. The signs are singing. We can see trees to the East. This looks more promising - and it is.

Across the world, people have perceived forest wildernesses to be full of spirit, as if the real and visible world had an equally real but invisible world folded within it.

Jay Griffiths *(Wild: An Elemental Journey,* p. 53).

It never ceases to amaze how, within a few short steps, the feeling of our surroundings can change completely. Guy Debord talks of moving between zones of distinct psychic atmospheres in the city. We believe that this can also happen outwith an urban setting as described in our post on the Fife Coastal Path. This happens here. One minute we are unmistakably in a quiet residential area of a small Fife town. Our most noticeable observation is a black cat dozing contentedly on top of a blue plastic dustbin. She jumps down to greet us and walks a few paces alongside glad of the company. A few steps later and we are through that transition zone and enter The Wilderness. It really does exist.

Tree mouth

It's good to feel the sun today. Fingers of warmth entwine and clasp hands amongst us. The lichens on my skin dissolve into light and the ivy loosens slightly. Stretching up towards the blue, a moment held in these short, chill days. Drinking from the earth, heavy with water. Sustained.

There are movers on the path. Coming.

Fingers of warmth entwine and clasp hands amongst us

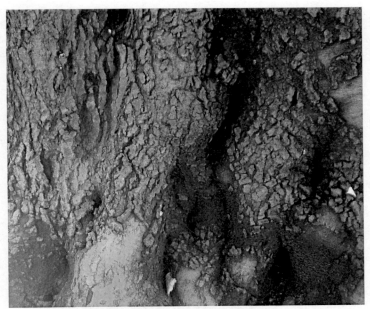

lichens on my skin dissolve into light

the ivy loosens slightly

We enter the invisible, folded, other world of the wood. Old trees, bark encrusted with mottled green. Root formations resemble clawed, long-toed dinosaur feet. We expect them to lift free from the ground at any time.

Hollowed out stumps of wooden teeth sup on leaves and sunlight.

There is a sense of a trail through the woods but little evidence of human visitation. During our visit no one arrives. No one goes. Just us. The trees and the sound and sense of birds. We find out later that there is no through-route. You have to climb a fence at the other end to get out so The Wilderness is effectively a bounded area. No doubt this discourages the use of the woods as path of transit, but perhaps helps to retain a little sliver of embedded wilderness.

We have often found that bounded, hidden areas become covert fly tipping sites but there is remarkably little evidence of this practice. A stray carrier bag probably relates to the two empty cans of Foster's lager tossed aside.

You can almost visualise the youngsters chipping in to scrape up enough money for their couple of cans before heading to the woods in anticipation of some bacchanalian wildness. We later find one car tyre and a bicycle frame. No white goods!

The purring murmur of running water soon entices and we follow the slope of the land down towards a wee burn.

Flowing here for many a year that's what us wee burns do. The flow and the flux of the present moment, always existing in the eternal now. No history, no future, no time. Old Heraclitus was right you never step in the same burn twice.

Burn, stream, river, estuary. It's all just a matter of scale.

A balloon lies trapped on the water underneath a branch. A human breath captured in time and space.

Imagine a situation where the last trace of human life on earth was the breath captured in a balloon? The most ephemeral of traces. Perhaps this is the breath of the Earth. The life-force slowly puckering, deflating, evaporating. If The Wilderness can exist in Rosyth, then why not the breath of Planet Earth?

We follow the burn through to the end of the wood, watched by the bug-eyed tree spirit. Chameleon eyes surveying, observing. Oblivious to time or circumstance.

Listening and watching the wildness of the fungi, spilling from the tree stump.

[L o s t t i m e i n t h e m o m e n t]

Over the fence at the other end and we are back in a residential street. We know that we are walking down the front leg of the cartoon fox. Appropriately, the road is called Burnside.

The paws of the fox mark the transition zone and we exit The Wilderness and track back through Rosyth past the Carnegie Institute.

Back to civilisation, the chimneys, the birds and the tags.

Rosyth Institute - the chimneys, the birds

Appendix: The Wilderness over time

The Wilderness 1915

1915 - The Wilderness and our Fox are fully formed.

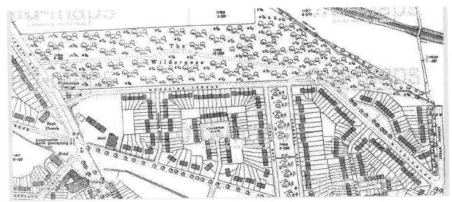

The Wilderness 1926-27

1926 -1927: The Garden City of Rosyth is now built. We can still see our fox although the rump has been annexed. A trail through The Wilderness is indicated on the map. Wilderness Cottage sits at the South West corner. Our best guess is that this was demolished and replaced by a new build church.

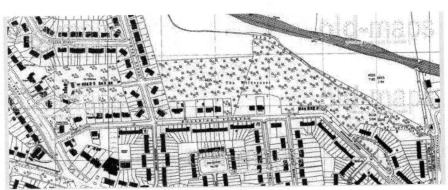

Wilderness 1952-66

1952-1966: New residential building has dissected our Fox's torso almost right through the middle.

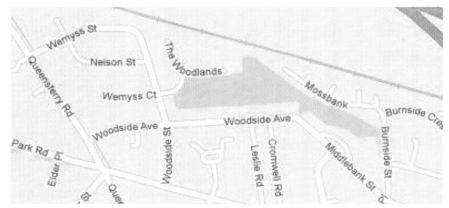

The Wilderness – 2013

2013: This is how The Wilderness is represented on Google Maps. Only a sliver of green remains - the head of our fox. The name has also disappeared but we know that however diminished it may be, The Wilderness most certainly does exist.

Now Playing: Andrew Chalk - The River that Flows into the Sands

16th January 2013

References:

Jay Griffiths, *Wild: An Elemental Journey* (London: Penguin Books, 2006).

Map extracts sourced through Old Maps UK

Zaha Hadid and Kirkcaldy

Zaha Hadid has recently won the The Stirling Prize for her National Museum of 21st Century Art, in Rome, which appears to resemble some sort of cubist Star Wars, AT-AT Walker.

For such a lauded and controversial architect (in Britain!) it is quite surprising to learn that she has only had two designs realised in the UK. The recently opened Evelyn Grace Academy in Brixton and her first built work, Maggie's Cancer Care Centre in Kirkcaldy which was opened in 2006.[1]

Hadid designed this building for no fee and the people of Fife, raised over £500,000 towards the cost of its construction.

The criticisms often levied against Hadid are that her designs focus on spectacle rather than the purely functional. She wants her buildings to look great rather than just do the utilitarian job and surely there is nothing wrong with that: "They should have an impact on the street life and they should draw people to them. They have to be interesting. I don't think everything should be the same and this obsession with sameness had to do with the industrial period of mass production and now we don't have to look at things like that." (*The Guardian*, 9th October 2010, p. 34).

---

[1] Correct at the time of writing. The Riverside Museum in Glasgow was opened in 2011.

Her design at the Victoria Hospital was a result of a brief to: 'create a relaxed atmosphere where people can access additional support outside of the more clinical hospital environment'. This challenge is in keeping with the ethos behind all the Maggie's Centres which were the vision of the late Maggie Keswick-Jencks and her plea to improve care for people with cancer in the UK. She was a firm believer in the capacity of buildings and space to uplift people, even in the most challenging personal circumstances. Her husband Charles Jencks is still actively carrying this vision forward and five centres, have now been constructed across the UK, all designed by world-renowned architects: Frank Gehry in Dundee, Daniel Libeskind in Cambridge, Page and Park Architects in Glasgow and Inverness and Zaha Hadid in Kirkcaldy.

The site of Hadid's Maggie's Centre is in a hollow to the south-west of the main entrance of the hospital where it stands on the edge of a fairly steep valley to the South. The hollow has overgrown foliage and a line of trees provides a natural setting to distance the building from the rest of the

221

original hospital. As the building is a single-storey construction, it provides a continuation of the border that the trees already provide. One of the overall objectives for the design of the centre was that it should be a transition between the two different types of spaces, the natural landscape and the car park/hospital. This has arguably been undermined somewhat by the colossal new 525 bed extension which has been built immediately adjacent to the centre and you can almost feel it crowding out and pushing Hadid's building into the valley. This is further accentuated by Hadid's design, with its angular prow and folded in wings, which appears to float over the edge of the steep chasm. Part spaceship, part cubist crow, poised to take flight out over the trees and on to the stars.

A truly liminal space...

Now playing: Oneohtrix Point Never – *Returnal*

11th October 2010

The Woods and the Words

The stories are still told

of a time before the water.

When the earth lay heaped,

black and smouldering.

It is said that they tunnelled

        u

        n

        d

        e

g   r   o   u   n   d

for black diamonds

to burn for warmth.

A structure survived

the darkest of

the dark days -

although, now, no one

is quite sure

what it was used for

Now.

now to simply be

amongst our co-dwellers

in this healing place.

If you remain still

for long enough

they become curious

and congregate,

silently swaying

with the wind.

A few season-cycles ago

the visitors started to return.

We listen for their arrival

always the calling first.

despite

bluebell

all that happened

stitchwort

the woods and the words

wild hyacinth

at least

oak

some of the words

hazel

and some of the woods

dog mercury

survive

And the thin

bleached light

of a pale sun

continues to shine

on the white tree

of Harran Hill Wood.

♦

♦

♦   ♦

♦

♦

This little field trip, possibly sent from another point in time (?), was inspired by frequent visits to a favorite place in Central Fife: Lochore Meadows or The Meedies as it is known locally.

The Meedies opened as a Country Park in 1976 following one of the largest and most ambitious industrial landscape renovation projects in Europe.

This included the reclamation of 600ha of heavily contaminated land comprising six redundant coal mine sites, colliery buildings, mineral railways, refuse tipping, areas of subsidence and the towering pit bings (most of them burning) which rose to 60m over the surrounding countryside and settlements.

The Meedies is now a major centre for outdoor and environmental education with Loch Ore the largest area of standing water in Fife. It is an important habitat for wildfowl with significant numbers both over-wintering and breeding. Otters, bats, water voles and even ospreys have been recorded within the park boundary. The acid grasslands of Clune Craig are botanically rich and also bear traces of hut-circles and enclosures from a Bronze age settlement.

The 'structure' in the photographs above is the reinforced concrete headframe of the 'Big Mary' No. 2 pit shaft, sunk in 1923. It is one of only two such surviving structures in Fife and a monument to the Kingdom's mining heritage. (The other is The Frances in Dysart). You can gain some impression of how the area looked when mining was in operation from this photograph:

The pit head is in the distance and the smouldering pit bings in the foreground. This photograph is from the fabulous web resource on the Fife Pits by Michael Martin which can be accessed here.

The original Loch Ore was drained in the 1790s when the landowner, Captain Parks, attempted to reclaim the land for cattle grazing. The project was a commercial failure and the land formerly occupied by the loch remained boggy. Parks was declared bankrupt in 1798. The loch gradually returned in the mid-20th century, when coal mining flourished and the mineral railway serving the pithead became an embankment surrounded by water. The return of the loch was mainly due to subsidence caused by mining, and the 'new' loch now occupies a different footprint to the original.

The loch is now stabilised but its depth still fluctuates. The islands in the loch are the remains of the former railway embankment.

To the north west lies Harran Hill Wood which sits on a rocky ledge between Loch Ore and Benarty Hill. Botanical studies indicate a strong possibility that this site may have been wooded since shortly after the last Ice Age c. 10,000 years ago.

Whilst writing this, I'm listening to a composed piece called *After The Rain* by Barry Guy, perhaps better known as a free improviser. I don't think I had ever read the sleeve notes before but was intrigued to learn that it was partly inspired by the Max Ernst painting *Europe After the Rain*. As Guy says in the sleeve notes:

"The canvas portrays four large masses of tortuous baroque-like remains as if left after some unfathomable catastrophe...these images invite the viewer to speculate on the nature of the events. Here in *Europe, After the Rain* could be the apotheosis of anxiety and destruction or the emergence of new life from the ruins. I am drawn to the latter..."

Now Playing: Barry Guy and City of London Sinfonia - *After the Rain*

15th November 2012

References:

Fife Council Lochore Meadows Country Park Development Plan, November 2008.

Michael Martin, *Fife Pits and Memorial Book*,
http://www.users.zetnet.co.uk/mmartin/fifepits/

Miles K Oglethorpe, (2006), *Scottish Collieries: An Inventory of the Scottish Coal Industry in the Nationalised Era* (Edinburgh, The Royal Commission on the Ancient and Historical Monuments of Scotland).

An Almost Supernatural Manifestation...

I must have taken this journey hundreds of times. The railway crossing over the Firth of Forth, rumbling through the three red diamonds of the Rail Bridge.

The train window frames a changing canvas of sea and sky as weather formations dance in constant flux. Bright, clear days offer sunlight stained, glassy blues which stretch to the horizon, punctuated by the islands of Inchcolm, Inchmickery and Inchkeith. The abandoned World War II fortifications of Inchgarvie, lie directly underneath the bridge. Hollowed out shells, windows like mouths of gaping teeth, now colonised by seabirds. The gulls ascend to hover on the updraughts, peering into the train window, before coasting off and plummeting seaward - racing gravity. On certain days, a tang of salt air permeates the hermetically sealed train carriage.

There is an excitement in looking out and observing the great diagonal smears of rain advancing up the estuary. Slabs of smudged grey - coming this way. Tumultuous skies billowing with angry clouds blown in by sea winds. The theatre of watching the weather arrive.

However, I have never experienced conditions such as observed this week. (Thursday 26th July c. 2.30 pm). A spectacular form of haar (coastal sea fog) appeared to manifest from nowhere on an otherwise relatively 'sunny day'. Not so much the haar rolling in but an almost supernatural manifestation.

From the railway bridge over the Forth

a blue-tinged wash of elemental greys.

Sea and sky bleed

into a Rothko memory

Taken just a few moments later, you can see some of the river tugs off to the right. The oil terminal at Hound Point is just emerging from the glaur, as the blue starts to break through again.

...

I posted the above photographs on twitter and a couple of days later Bob Reid sent me this one. Same place, different time.

The Forth: always different, always the same.

© Bob Reid with thanks

Now playing: James Yorkston - *When the Haar Rolls In*.

28th July 2013

Marking Time (with assorted Rag-Pickings & essays)

Is this the first published use of the term 'psychogeography'?

"The science of anthropogeography, or more properly speaking, psychogeography, deals with the influence of geographical environment on the human mind."

J. Walter Fewkes, Bureau of American Ethnology, (1905)

≈≈≈

CLIMATE AND CULT

By J. WALTER FEWKES, Bureau of American Ethnology

The science of anthropogeography, or, more properly speaking, psychogeography, deals with the influence of geographical environment on the human mind. The effect appears in that responsive expression of mind which is known as culture. Evolution of culture

Presented in a paper 'Climate and Cult' published in the *Report of the Eighth International Geographic Congress*. 1904, pp.664-670, (Washington: Washington Government Printing Office, 1905).

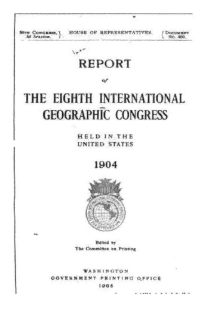

Jesse Walter Fewkes (1850 - 1930) was born in Newton, Massachusetts and initially pursued a career as a marine zoologist at Harvard. From 1887, he turned his attention to anthropology and ethnological studies, particularly the culture and history of the Pueblo Native Americans. Fewkes made some of the first recordings of their music. In 1895 he embarked on various archaeological explorations of the American Southwest for the Smithsonian's Bureau of American Ethnology. In 1918 he was appointed chief of the Bureau and retired in 1928, dying two years later.

The paper Fewkes presented to the Congress examines the relationship between climate, food supply and ritual ceremony, (what Fewkes calls 'cult').

237

One example given is the rain ceremonies of the Hopi people. Fewkes argues that the Hopi's strong connection with their arid landscape led them to develop a set of beliefs, practices and rituals to appeal to the sky gods to deliver rain. In these ceremonies, the gods are represented through masks, idols and other symbols and in order to influence the "magic powers of these personages" the worshipper employs signs or gestures, songs, verbal incantations or rituals of imitation. For example, water is poured into a medicine bowl from its four sides to show that water is desired from all world quarters; a cloud of smoke represents a rain cloud. Sacred kivas (rooms used for rituals) are painted with symbols of falling rain and lightning to remind the gods of the Hopi people's need for water.

As a conference paper, it is very much of its time but interesting in that it specifically mentions 'psychogeography' and clearly relates this to a linkage between the effect of the environment on the human mind. We have never seen it referenced before in any of the psychogeographic literature.

References to the origin of the term 'psychogeography' often refer to Guy Debord's *Introduction to a Critique of Urban Geography,* (1955) and his definition:

Psychogeography sets for itself the study of the precise laws and specific effects of the geographical environment, whether consciously organised or not, on the emotions and behavior of individuals.

Whilst the Letterists and Situationists clearly developed their psychogeographic activities, during the 1950s, in an urban environment, it is interesting to learn that the relationship between the environment and the human mind was being considered as 'psychogeography' in a non-urban context at the turn of the century.

Now playing: Éliane Radigue - *Elemental II.*

30th October 2014

Poem for Ralph Rumney

Poor Pegeen   Rumney

                 on   the

           r----------U---------n   Peggy

Guggenheim..............in............ purrr.................... s....u...i..t

       He

c#h#e#c#k#s

                         in with **Guattari**

at La Borde

          a fellow patient and former welder

      breaks Rumney's **2CV** into

           p   ie

            c

           es

     to make a sculpture

"Something I thought was rather brilliant. I appreciated that very much"
(1)

Reference:

(1). Ralph Rumney, (2002), *The Consul*, (San Francisco: City Light Books), p. 96.

Now playing: Ambarchi and Brinkmann - *The Mortimer Trap**

11th April 2012

Threshold

trying

                  to catch

                                    a thread

                 of time

when

              theincomingtide

                                  becomes

the o u t g o i n g t i d e

listening

                                                    ebb

         listening for

   flow

                         an inflexion

                            ebb

       of breath

   flow

inhalation

                            ebb

      becoming

   flow

exhalation

     flow

    exhalation

          ebb

becoming

     flow

    inhalation

          ebb

at the river

still standing

grounded

still standing grounded

at the river, still standing grounded - but different

Now playing: The Necks – *Silverwater*

9th August 2012

Plants, Potters, Webs: On Forms, Usefulness and Emptiness

With the clocks about to go back this weekend, autumnal hues cloak the body and seep into the skin. The piercing light of summer is almost emptied out. Weak threads of sunlight dissolve amongst russet, ochre and blanket skies of grey.

Here then, some small cups of blue:

inked

        upon the sky

blue

        cupped

time

        held

in a breath

≈≈≈

The potter makes the earthen pitcher out of earth selected and prepared specifically for it. The potter ... shapes the clay. No - he shapes the emptiness.

Martin Heidegger

When posting the above image on twitter, I received, by return, a digital echo from Andrew Male, (@AndrewMaleMojo). A fragile image, of the same unknown plant, etched in glaze and fire; 'cupped' and bleeding into blue.

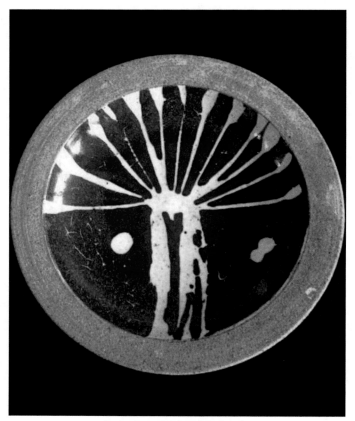

© Andrew Male with thanks

The bowl was made by the potter Beresford Pealing who ran a studio-pottery at Harnham Mill, West Harnham, Salisbury, Wiltshire from 1966-1972. Pealing created hand-thrown domestic stoneware of a type pioneered by Bernard Leach working in an Arts & Crafts tradition.

Beresford Pealing's studio-pottery at Harnham Mill. © Wiltshire Museums

The image of Pealing's bowl resonated with the image of that flower cupping light, sky and time and somehow reminded me of Martin Heidegger's late thought, particularly his Bremen Lecture of 1949, *Insight into That Which Is:*

When we fill the pitcher, the liquid flows into the empty pitcher ... The thingness of the container in no way rests in the material that it is made of, but in the emptiness that [it?] contains.

I'm not sure if Heidegger ever acknowledged it, but it seems too much of a coincidence if this passage was not influenced by the arguably more poetic rendering in the *Tao Te Ching:*

Shape clay into a vessel;
It is the space within that makes it useful.

(*Tao Te Ching*: Chapter 11, translated by Stephen Mitchell, 1988)

or in an alternative translation:

Hollowed out,
clay makes a pot.
Where the pot's not
is where it's useful.

(*Tao Te Ching*: Chapter 11, translated by Ursula K. Le Guin, 1998)

A random moment this week threaded together that plant inked against the sky and Beresford Pealing's bowl. Opening the front door, an empty form cupping the autumn light:

Overnight, a dweller on the threshold had constructed possibly the perfect form of useful emptiness. A filigree construction allowing the world to pass through and bring whatever bounty may stick on the way...

And of the unknown plant?

When the photograph was taken, I had no idea what it was, although A, who is the gardener, told me that it would soon 'explode'. She didn't know the name either. Fraser MacDonald @JAFMacDonald kindly identified it as *Agapanthus* and sent a link to a stunning time-lapse film of white stars exploding in all their glory. All within fifteen seconds.

But there is one final act of synchronicity. Re-watching the film clip today and revisiting Heidegger's lecture, I come across his thinking on the emerging technologies of 1949 (for example film) and specifically, their ability to collapse time and space. An example that he gives is:

the sprouting and flourishing of plants which remained hidden throughout the seasons is now openly displayed on film within a minute...

We can only imagine what his response may have been to the webs spun by modern technologies. Lots of *un-useful* emptiness? Perhaps we can learn from the spider. Spin the web, shape the emptiness and see what sticks.

Many thanks go to Andrew Male and Fraser MacDonald for their invaluable contributions to this post.

Now playing: Brian Lavelle - *Empty Transmissions.*

25th October 2014

References:

Martin Heidegger, *Insight into That Which Is,* Bremen Lecture, 1949 (Indiana: Indiana University Press, 2012)

Lao Tzu. *The Tao Te Ching,* various translations.

Wheel of Life

retired tyre

wheel of life

30th September 2014

Fife Folk-Lore: Cures for Whooping Cough and Other Ailments

Publications of The Folk-Lore Society LXXI. (Detail)

Cures for Whooping Cough:

(1) Passing the child under the belly of a donkey;

(2) Carrying the child until you meet a rider on a white (or a piebald) horse, and asking his advice: what he advises has to be done;

(3) Taking the child to a lime-kiln;

(4) Taking the child to a gas-works. During an outbreak of whooping-cough in 1891, the children of the man in charge of, and living at, a gas works did not take the complaint. As a matter of fact, the air in and near a gas-works contains pyridin, which acts as an antiseptic and a germicide;

(5) Treating the child with roasted mouse-dust;

(6) Getting bread and milk from a woman whose married surname was the same as her maiden one;

(7) Giving the patient a sudden start.

Breathing the smell of freshly dug earth was held to be good for whooping-cough, and also for those who had been poisoned with bad air. A hole was dug in the ground and the patient "breathed the air off it." A "divot" of turf was sometimes, in the old days, cut and placed on the pillow.

249

How to get rid of Warts:

(1) Rubbing with a slug and impaling the slug on a thorn. As the slug decays the warts go;

(2) Rubbing with a piece of stolen meat, as the meat decays the warts go;

(3) Tying as many knots on a piece of string as there are warts, and burying the string. As the string decays the warts go;

(4) Take a piece of straw and cut it into as many pieces as there are warts, either bury them or strew them to the winds;

(5) Dip the warts into the water-tub where the smith cools the red-hot horse-shoes in the smithy;

(6) Dip the warts in pig's blood when the pig is killed.

Piles are treated by:

(1) sitting over a pail containing smouldering burnt leather;

(2) the application of used axle-grease.

All of the above from County Folk-Lore Vol VII. Examples of Printed Folk-Lore concerning Fife with some notes on Clackmannan and Kinross-Shires collected by John Ewart Simpkins (London: Sidgwick & Jackson for the Folk-Lore Society, 1914).

Now Playing: The Owl Service and Alison O'Donnell - *The Fabric of Folk*

12ᵗʰ June 2013

Solstice

On the longest day

        all

           hail the light

≈

21 June 2014. Walking along an overgrown railway track near Crombie in Fife. As 'night' approaches, darkness fails to smother the light. Even the Giant Hogweed (?) appears to embrace the sky.

Now playing: Loren Mazzacane & Suzanne Langille - *Come Night*

22nd June 2014

An Irrevocable Brilliance: Guy Debord in the Landscape

Debord's house at Champot, (c) Luc Olivier

I have had no need to travel very far

In Guy Debord's autobiography, *Panegyric*, he describes having spent the greater part of his life in Paris, specifically within the triangle defined by the intersections of rue Saint-Jacques and rue Royer-Collard; rue Saint-Martin and rue Greneta; and rue du Bac and rue de Commailles.

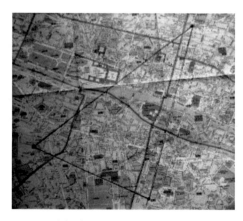

Never or hardly ever, would I have left this area which suited me perfectly. However, for the last 20 years of his life, Debord spent increasing amounts of time in an isolated house at Champot Haut, situated in Bellevue-la-Montagne, a commune (population c. 500) in the Haute-

253

Loire *département* of the Auvergne. From 1975 onwards, Debord spent most summers and a few winters there with his second wife Alice Becker-Ho.

The idea of Debord as a Landscape writer is not one that would immediately spring to mind, yet over a few pages in *Panegyric*, Debord paints a lyrical elegy to the natural world and landscape of Champot.

Inaccessible • isolated • surrounded by woods

I have even stayed in an inaccessible house surrounded by woods, far from any village, in an extremely barren, exhausted mountainous region, deep in a deserted Auvergne. I spent several winters there.

snow • drifts • logs • fire

Snow would fall for days on end. The wind piled it up in drifts. Barriers kept it off the road. Despite the surrounding walls, snow accumulated in the courtyard. Logs were piled high on the fire.

at night • an opening to the Milky Way • stars so close

The house seemed to open directly onto the Milky Way. At night, the stars, so close, would shine brilliantly one moment, and the next be extinguished by the passing mist...

a land of storms • horizon flashes • under siege

It was a land of storms. They would approach silently at first, announced by the brief passage of a wind that slithered through the grass or by a series of sudden flashes on the horizon; then thunder and lightning would be unleashed, and we would be bombarded for a long while from every direction, as if in a fortress under siege.

a lightning strike • an illuminated landscape • an irrevocable brilliance

Just once, at night, I saw lightning strike near me outside: you could not even see where it had struck; the whole landscape was equally illuminated for one startling instant. Nothing in art has ever given me this impression of an irrevocable brilliance, except for the prose that Lautréamont employed in the programmatic exposition that he called Poésies...

high winds • shaken trees • relentless assault

High winds which at any moment could rise from one of three directions, shook the trees. The more dispersed trees on the heath to the north dipped and shook like ships surprised at anchor in an unprotected harbour. The compactly grouped trees that guarded the hillock in front of the house supported one another in their resistance, the first rank breaking the west wind's relentless assault...

clouds traverse the sky • winds retreat • relaunch

Masses of clouds traversed the sky at a run. A sudden change of wind could also quickly send them into retreat, with other clouds launched in their pursuit.

all the birds • chill of air • shades of green • tremulous light

On calm mornings, there were all the birds of the dawn and the perfect chill of air, and that dazzling shade of tender green that came over the trees, in the tremulous light of the sun rising before them...

the arrival of autumn • a sweetness in the air • 'the first breath of spring'

The weeks went by imperceptibly. One day the morning air would announce the arrival of autumn. Another time, a great sweetness in the air, a sweetness you could taste, would declare itself, like a quick promise always kept, 'the first breath of spring.'

in the square • extraordinary encounters • the owl of Minerva

In the midwinter nights of 1988, in the Square des Missions Étrangères, an owl would obstinately repeat his calls, fooled perhaps by the unseasonal weather. And this extraordinary series of encounters with the bird of Minerva, its atmosphere of surprise and indignation, did not in the least seem to constitute an allusion to the imprudent conduct or the various aberrations of my life. I have ever understood where my life could have been different or how it ought to be justified.

a pleasing and impressive solitude

It was a pleasing and impressive solitude. But to tell the truth, I was not alone: I was with Alice.

At Champot, on 30th November 1994, Guy Debord shot himself through the heart with a single bullet.

Now playing: Jean-Claude Eloy - Chants pour l'autre moitié du ciel / Songs for the other half of the sky.

5th June 2014

References:

Guy Debord, Panegyric Volumes 1 & 2, translated by James Brook and John McHale (London: Verso, 2004).

Frozen Motion: Topographies of Ice

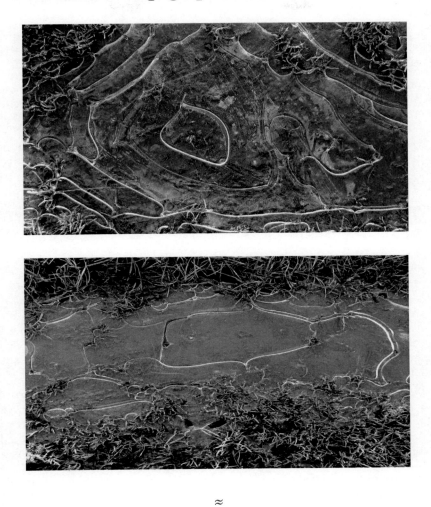

≈

Now playing: Thomas Köner - 'Meta Incognita' from *Permafrost*.

11th January 2015

By Leaves We Live - From Geddes to Monbiot

An interesting article from George Monbiot recently in *The Guardian* which taps into the FPC's interest in the great visionary generalist and ecologist Patrick Geddes.

Monbiot's piece of 10th August, *('We have allowed developers to rob us of our village green')* recounts a camping trip to an 'ordinary campsite' where the tents were situated around a square field. He observed the curious effect this had on the children staying there. Drawn towards the centre of field, children of all classes started playing together and engaging in communal activities whilst the parents started talking to each other. As Monbiot says: "it hit me with some force: we had reinvented the village green". The key point of his anecdote is that: "we are, to a surprising extent, what the built environment makes us".

Inspired by this, Monbiot performs a trawl on related research papers which include conclusions such as:

- People's use of shared spaces is strongly influenced by trees: the more there are, the more people spend time there;
- Vegetation in common spaces increases social ties;
- Social isolation is commonly associated with an absence of green spaces;
- Wealthy parts of a city usually have tree cover of c.10%. Poor neighbourhoods just 2%.

Monbiot's main contention is that we have allowed property developers and weak planning to define who we are and what we shall become. His prescription is pretty simple. Houses or apartment blocks should be built around a square of shared green space. It should be big enough for playing ball games, contain trees and rocks or logs to climb on and perhaps a corner of uncut meadow or flowerbeds and fruit bushes. The space will work best when it is designed and managed by the people who live there. Most important is that the houses face inwards and no cars can access the square. The space is overlooked by everyone which means that children can run in and out of houses, unsupervised and create their own tribes.

The point that struck me most about Monbiot's article is that almost all of his arguments were made equally forcibly in theory and practice by Patrick Geddes in the Old Town of Edinburgh in the late 1800s.

The themes that emerge in all of Geddes's work include a pioneering, ecological approach to cities and their problems; arguments for self-management, decentralisation, and the need for co-operative mutual aid. As Jonathan Porritt, the Green activist has commented:

'For me he is one of those pioneers of what we now call sustainable development'.

During the 1880s, Geddes, was a lecturer of zoology at Edinburgh University and contributing entries to the Britannica and Chambers Encyclopaedias on scientific subjects whilst his range of interests had widened so that he was now publishing papers on subjects such as Statistics, Economics, Art Criticism, and Co-Operation as a political philosophy. Interestingly, after having studied with T.H. Huxley - 'Darwin's bulldog' - Geddes did not subscribe to the tooth and claw, survival of the fittest doctrine. Like his friend Peter Kropotkin, Geddes considered mutual aid and co-operation as equally evident in the natural world - for example in the bee colony.

In his spare time, Geddes assembled a collective of like-minded individuals to form an presciently named Environment Society which began a series of urban interventions using the Old Town of Edinburgh as a 'social laboratory' to develop both his social thought and to engage in practical social action. This was against the backdrop of the Old Town having some of the worst living conditions in Europe at the time and the observation was not lost on Geddes that the rent payments of the impoverished Old Town tenants helped to maintain the comfortable citizenry on the other side of Princes Street in the New Town.

Three months after marriage to Anna Morton, Geddes and his wife moved from the New Town into James Court in the Old Town. James Court was a six-storey tenement housing some twenty-five families, primarily in single rooms, located on a common stair. This initiative allowed the Geddeses to acquire intimate knowledge of how slum dwellers were actually affected by their surroundings and what could be most readily done to improve them. The occupants of James Court were filled with a population belonging to the lower ranks of skilled labour including cobblers, blacksmiths and chimney sweeps. At first, the Geddeses were viewed with suspicion, but with customary zeal, they began the practical transformation of their immediate environment. His daughter, Nora, has recounted how Geddes quickly mobilised the tenement residents into clearing, whitewashing and window gardening.

In 1884, Geddes formed the Edinburgh Social Union ("ESU") and it was Anna Geddes who encouraged Patrick Geddes to take cognisance of the philanthropic housing work being undertaken in London by Octavia Hill with the support of John Ruskin. To give a sense of scale, beginning with two properties in 1885, by 1897, the ESU was responsible for managing 23 properties housing 450 families. It is also worth stressing that many of these properties would have been demolished by the municipal authorities without the intervention of the Social Union and Geddes's practice of Conservative Surgery, which he likened to pruning the branches of a tree. What this meant was the preservation of old, structurally sound, buildings and transforming them into clean and usable habitations with rents maintained at levels that the working classes could afford.

From the outset, Social Union funds were also used for window box gardens and flower shows and art classes were given to 'help to render homes beautiful'. These classes included: wood-carving, brass beating, stencilling, mosaic, and leather stamping. Entertainments were given in a number of properties on Saturday evenings consisting of music, recitations, magic lantern entertainments and tableaux. Libraries were also installed in many properties. Geddes as Head of the ESU art committee was also responsible for the introduction of decorative art into various public buildings. Some were quite modest such as reproducing Millais' *Parables* in a Grassmarket Mission Hall whilst a history of corn in six panels was commissioned from the young Edinburgh Artist Charles Mackie. One of the major projects undertaken was the decoration of the mortuary chapel of the Sick Children's hospital undertaken by Phoebe Traquair in 1885. Also, as Glendinning and Page say, Geddes 'almost single handedly set about the revival of mural painting in Scotland in the hope that decorating homes, schools and workplaces with scenes of national history and legend might help regenerate modern materialistic society'.

The important point about all these initiatives were that they were *visible* to the tenement inhabitants. As Geddes would later write: 'to improve the condition of the people, the improvement must be on a scale that they can observe and realised; not frittered away piecemeal as are so many municipal improvements'.

Geddes's initiatives in James Court were rooted in direct action from within the community and locality. His interventions were not party political but a recognition that the future depended upon creating the self-awareness and determination of the community at large in the development of the city'.

Geddes also began to provide University Halls of residence for students, which was unique in Britain, in that it was entirely self-governing with no warden or master. Students were required to co-operate and take mutual responsibility for its operation and student numbers increased to over 200. This initiative was part of Geddes's vision of using the University as a means of cultural renewal and his objective was to bring students back to live in the Old Town where the great eighteenth century scholars had lived. This initiative also attracted a core of student acolytes to help him in his work and the spirit of this initiative was encapsulated in Geddes's motto for the Hall: *Vivendo Discimus* – 'by living we learn'.

Geddes's always considered himself to be a garden-maker and the creation of gardens is a recurring feature of his urban initiatives throughout the world. For Geddes 'the garden' was an educational tool and apart from the aesthetic qualities he considered it as the 'very best of savings banks, for in return for deposits of time and strength, the worker reaps health for themselves, and their children in air, in vegetables and in fruit'. They were also social spaces that brought people together and humanised the urban environment. Geddes's Environment Society began to cultivate waste ground by making small gardens and planting trees, trying to encourage the tenement dwellers into a dynamic relationship with their environment. This was at the core of Geddes's approach to urban social problems. Engaging folk with place to encourage an active and dynamic relationship with their environment.

I'm sure that George Monbiot would approve.

Now Playing: Ben Frost: *Theory of Machines*

26th August 2010

NOW SING (and soothe the city fabric)

Whilst in Glasgow recently, it was a sad sight to walk along Renfield Street and see the hollowed out shell of The Glasgow School of Art. Even in its fire-damaged condition, Charles Rennie Mackintosh's architectural masterpiece remains identifiable as one of the great buildings of the world.

On the other side of the street, a shiny new neighbour, the Reid Building, hunches over its ailing, elderly companion. A reflective sympathy of glass, metal and concrete. On the balcony, Michael Stumpf's installation, speaking to the moment:

As an invocation, it's a good one:

NOW SING

As twilight descends, and the sounds of Sauchiehall Street murmur below, we can imagine the Reid Building and all people passing, singing soft lullabies. Songs to comfort. Songs to bring back light and air to soot-blackened lungs. Songs to soothe the city fabric.

So no fire damaged pictures of The Mackintosh Building. Its presence will always be there: to heal, challenge and sustain the human imagination, whatever its material state.

(and soothe the city fabric)

Now playing: Richard Youngs - 'The Future is So Different Today' from *Summer Through My Mind*

9th July 2014

The Last Sound of an Echo

somewhere between Charlestown and Dunfermline

                              an   e c h o

the   s o u n d

             s o u n d   of

the   last   s o u n d

the   e c h o

the   s o u n d   of   an   e c h o

the   last   e c h o

the   last   s o u n d   of   an   e c h o

             s o u n d   o

      s   o u n

             d   o   n   e

≈

Now playing: Pauline Oliveros, Stuart Dempster, Panaiotis - *Deep Listening*
4th May 2014

I Remember (after Brainard and Perec)

The starting point is George Perec's *Je Me Souviens* (1978) which I instantly fell in love with on a visit to Paris. I literally stumbled across it in a small bookshop, in the 7th *arrondissement*. Books were stacked and littered on every available surface, including the floor. An ill placed foot brought one of the teetering towers tumbling down, and as I got down on hands and knees, muttering apologies in my pathetic French, this was the last book to go on the hastily reconstructed pile.

Each entry begins: "*Je me souviens...*" ("I remember...") followed by a snapshot of memory from Perec's everyday life. A sublime juxtaposition of the most casual banalities and epigramatic utterances. I subsequently read that Perec forced himself 'to remember' as a type of (anti) intellectual exercise and it is a book that makes you ponder on the small and seemingly inconsequential memories that give more resonance and ballast to existence than the dreary chronology of events that can reduce a life to a CV.

I later found out that Perec had adapted *Je me souviens* from Joe Brainard's book *I Remember* (1970). Brainard (1941 - 1994) was a prolific visual artist and writer associated with the New York School poets. Friend of Frank O'Hara, Larry Rivers, Jasper Johns and Andy Warhol. Paul Auster considers *I Remember* as "a masterpiece... one of the few totally original books I have ever read," whilst John Ashbery wrote that Brainard "proves that beauty is really interesting after all."

The idea behind *Je me Souviens/I Remember* is simple and so in the spirit, of Perec and Brainard here are a few:

1

I remember we lived for a short time in Victoria Avenue Milnathort, whilst we waited for our house in the New Town of Glenrothes to be 'finished'. I was out with my sister, walking hand in hand, to the little shop at the end of the street. I must have been three or four years old. It was very dark and as we swooped our torch around - there it was. Cowering against the side of the wall, a green budgie.

2

I remember being taken to see my Auntie Gertie. Hair scraped back, pencilled eyebrows, fur coat, smoking cigarettes and her thick German accent. I remember being told the story of how my Uncle Wullie met Gertie. He tripped over her dog coming out of a pub in Berlin: "What a braw wee dug".

3

I remember a particular room in my gran and granda's house. A musty old smell, a stuffed badger with menacing teeth. War medals. A copy of *Kidnapped* with colour plates which I liked to look at. A light that gave the illusion of water flowing when it was switched on.

4

I remember moving house from Milnathort to Glenrothes - the van broke down near Scotlandwell.

5

I remember running around outside carrying a milk bottle. I fell and the bottle shattered with a lot of glass ending up in my hand. The doctor pulled it out with tweezers. I remember a shard coming out four years later when I was eight years old. It had travelled an inch and part of it was resting against a tendon in my wrist. "It's been in there for half your life the doctor said". That evening, I remember watching a TV programme which had a rogue tiger pacing through rice fields, attacking and terrifying the local village.

6

I remember running away from home. I gathered up some things in a plastic carrier bag and matter of factly, told my parents I was running away. I went out the back door, no doubt being followed. I walked around the block and came in the front door, quite satisfied with my liberating adventure.

7

I remember the day my brother was brought home from the hospital after being born. I got a *Man from Uncle* car. You pressed a button on the roof and Napoleon Solo and Illya Kuryakin would come of the window as if shooting their guns.

8

I remember our first house in the new town of Glenrothes, Rimbleton precinct. All the precincts were named after the old farms on which the mass housing was built. Rimbleton streets were named after Scottish rivers: Clyde Court, Tay Court, Laxford Road, Moray Place...

I remember our second house in Glenrothes, Caskieberran precinct. All the streets had some connection to Sir Walter Scott: Marmion Drive, Waverley Drive, Kenilworth Court, Abbotsford Drive. Wonder what Barthes would have made of these signifiers?

I remember the concrete hippos and mushrooms which dwelt amongst the precincts and parks. For some reason their presence invoked a sense of comfort and made people smile. They were created by the town's public artist which sounded like a good job to have.

I remember my morning paper round. Up at 6.00am, almost every day of the year. Rain, hail, sleet, slush, snow and sunshine. A liberating sense of freedom, moving through the landscape before the town had woken up. Dark cloaked mornings in winter, beautiful fingers of light in summer.

I remember I had to deliver one copy of *The Financial Times*. It would sit like a slice of pink luncheon meat sandwiched within the gray tower of *Daily Records* and *Couriers*. It was for a Mr Mason, who, many years later, I discovered was the father of the Poll Tax.

I remember our one day wildcat strike at the R.S. McColl paper shop. It was planned for maximum impact on a Thursday when the local paper - *The Glenrothes Gazette* - came out. We ended up being interviewed by *The Gazette* and made the front page the following week. Our pay was increased from £1.25 a week to £1.75 a week. Result!

14

I remember that following the paper round pay rise, I could buy an album every second week.

Now Playing: Alog – *Unemployed*

11th January 2012

Walking Score No 1 (After Klee)

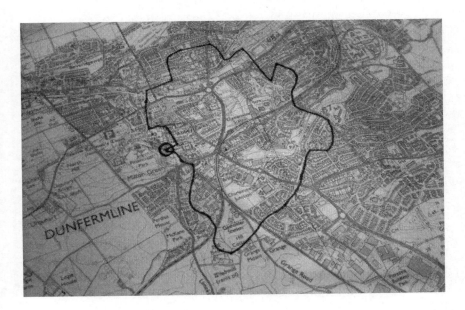

taking a line for a walk ~ Paul Klee

taking a walk on a line ~ FPC

~

Take a map drawn to any scale

~

Draw a line that starts and ends at the same place

~

Attempt to walk the line as far as is practicable

~

Record your experience in some form and share if desired

~

Paul Klee - Revolution des Viadukts, (1937)

Now Playing: Wire - *Map Ref. 41°N 93°W*

15th May 2013

On Samhain

The moon gazed on my midnight labours, while, with unrelaxed and breathless eagerness, I pursued nature to her hiding-places.

Mary Shelley

at the cusp of light and darkness

through veil of in-world and out-world

they arrive.

~~~

And if in Edinburgh look to the skies:

Witches over Edinburgh (1923).

Endpiece from *Dramatisations of History: The Masque of Ancient Learning and Its Many Meanings* by Patrick Geddes, Edinburgh: Patrick Geddes and Colleagues, (1923).

Now Playing: Rhys Chatham - *A Rite for Samhain* (From *The Bern Project*).

31st October 2012

Through Fence and Over Field

through fence

and over field - to

beyond the hem

of trees.

≈

Thanks to all who have taken time to read any of the postings this year. It has been much appreciated and a delight to interact with so many creative and interesting folk. Whether you chose to celebrate, or not, best wishes to all for a peaceful and enjoyable week and onwards to new openings and possibilities for Year 2013.

And just having a look at what Henry David Thoreau was writing in his journal on 24th December 1841:

I want to go soon and live away by the pond, where I shall hear only the wind whispering among the reeds. It will be success if I shall have left myself behind. But my friends ask what I will do when I get there. Will it not be employment enough to watch the progress of the seasons?

Walden Pond

Now playing: Jan Bang, Erik Honoré - *Uncommon Deities*. (With David Sylvian, Sidsel Endresen, Arve Henriksen, John Tilbury & Philip Jeck).

24th December 2012

Reference:

The Journal, 1837-1861 by Henry David Thoreau; preface by John R. Stilgoe, edited by Damion Searls (New York: New York Review Books classics, 2009).

Silently ... Being ... Silent

silently

      being

           silent

           ~

           being

      silent

silently

Now playing: Eliane Radigue - *Transamorem – Transmortem*

22nd July 2012

On experiencing a Live Performance of Morton Feldman's Coptic Light

A sounded weave 'pedals'
on spectral slubs of
small differences.

Time's flow, slows, to stasis
a colour field revealed,
in asymmetries of warp and weft.

There is no horizon here - only
a fullness of field, the patterning
of an essence, stretched
into aura.

All around is sound

All here is light.

≈

Coptic Light (1985) is a late work by Morton Feldman which was first performed by the New York Philharmonic, in 1986, just a year before he died. In many ways, C*optic Light* is an atypical late-Feldman piece, lasting just under thirty minutes. His major compositions from 1977 onwards had been exploring longer - and some would say extreme - duration with the vast sonic canvases of *For Christian Wolff* (1986) at around three hours; *For Philip Guston* (1984) lasting over four hours and *String Quartet No. 2* (1983) clocking in at up to six hours.

In *Give My Regards to Eighth Street* (2000), Feldman reveals some of his inspirations for *Coptic Light*. Commenting on an earlier composition, *Crippled Symmetry*, (1983) Feldman notes how his growing interest in Middle Eastern rugs had made him question what is symmetrical and what is not. In particular, he noticed the great variations in shades of colour in the rugs, as a result of the yarn having been dyed in small quantities. Similarly, the mirror image and patterns in many of these rugs was characterised by small variations and less concern with the exact accuracy of replication. This prompted Feldman to think of a disproportionate symmetry in repeating patterns - "a conscious attempt at formalizing a disorientation of memory".

Writing about *Coptic Light,* Feldman expresses his "avid interest in all varieties of arcane weaving of the Middle East" and in particular the stunning examples of early Coptic textiles on permanent display in The Louvre. What struck Feldman about these fragments of coloured cloth was "how they conveyed an essential atmosphere of their civilization". Applying this idea to his music, he asked himself what aspects of music, since

273

Monteverdi, might determine its atmosphere if heard two thousand years from now.

An important technical aspect of the composition was prompted by Sibelius's observation that the orchestra differs from the piano in that it has no pedal. Feldman therefore set out to create an 'orchestral pedal' continually varying in nuance. This *chiaroscuro* is both the compositional and instrumental focus of *Coptic Light*.

In this particular concert, *Coptic Light* was performed alongside Charles Ives's *The Unanswered Question,* (1906), which was perhaps the perfect choice. Two great American explorers, of the sonic landscape, bookending the 20th Century. Ives's own subtitle for *The Unanswered Question* was *'A Cosmic Landscape'*. As the plaintive trumpet intones and repeats 'The Perennial Question of Existence', The Question remains Unanswered and eventually all fades to silence.

Now Playing: Morton Feldman - *Coptic Light.* New World Symphony Orchestra conducted by Michael Tilson Thomas

19th September 2012

Reference:

Give My Regards to Eighth Street: Collected Writings of Morton Feldman, edited and with an introduction by B.H. Friedman, afterword by Frank O'Hara (Boston: Exact Change, 2000).

4'33" on a train - John Cage Centennial, 5th September 2012

Our modest contribution to the John Cage centennial celebrations. On 5th September 2012, we decided to undertake a performance of 4'33"on the train from Falkirk High to Glasgow Queen Street. Raising and lowering the seat tray served to mark the three movements. During our 'silent' performance this is what we heard:

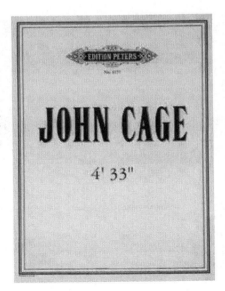

Low bas**S**   throb

                    - of tra**i**n thrum.

occasiona**l**>>>>>stabs

                    - of pitch**e**d track squeal.

                    a sigh
                    a cough

                    a s**n**eeze.
earphones fizzzzz and

            Crisps **C**runch.

        fingers tap on digital scr**e**ens
        as turning pages   - fan
            distant carriage whispers.

The **S**huddering recoil - fr**O**m

                        - the slap of a passing train

all so**U**nd and silence cocooned

                    - u**n**derneath a bridge.

Out in the lan**d**scape

            - an imagined Will**i**ams Mix:

        Doppler-shifted sire**n**,

    birdson**g** and turbine whirr.

        a rattttttttttttttling window
            "tickets please"
                tacet
            the seat tray creaks.

Happy 100th birthday John Cage. In another place you are walking around Walden Pond with Henry Thoreau looking for mushrooms.

Now Playing: John Cage and David Tudor - Rainforest II / Mureau - A Simultaneous Performance (Part I)

5th September 2012

What Can Happen on a Walk

```
walk
mind
body
senses
opening
mind body
senses
opening
being    in
world
opening
walk
mind    body
senses
opening
being       in
world    opening
walk
mind    body
senses  opening
m  b    i  o   n   d   d   y
b  w   e  o   i   r   n   l  g   d
```

Now playing: Oren Ambarchi - *Audience of One*
8th February 2012

Of Walking in Ice - Werner Herzog, Kenneth White and Liminal Pilgrimage

If I actually make it, no one will know what this journey means.

I'm following a direct imaginary line.

Werner Herzog's *Of Walking in Ice* is arguably one of the great texts of existential walking and pilgrimage. A short diary, never intended for publication, all is reduced to the (a)lone figure of Herzog moving through a landscape, trying to cope with a litany of physical discomforts and atrocious weather conditions which write themselves on his body. If psychogeography is an increasingly used, abused, and slippery signifier, it is clearly absent from Herzog's practice. There are no *dérives* here. This is walking as an act of resistance against the ultimate inevitability of death and as a process to absorb and internalise the landscape rather than make any attempt to open up and engage with it. This is an immersion into the mind and soul of the "I" pitted against malevolent nature that cares little for humankind.

I set off on the most direct route to Paris, in full faith, believing that she would stay alive if I came on foot. Besides I wanted to be alone with myself.

In November 1974, Herzog received a telephone call from a friend advising him that the German film critic Lotte Eisner was seriously ill and would 'probably die'. She was 78 years old. Herzog responds: "I said that this must not be, not at this time, German cinema could not do without her now, we would not permit her death". As an act of secular faith, he decides to walk from Munich to Paris and strides out on what turns out to be a three-week odyssey. Armed only with a jacket, compass, duffel bag, *new* boots (!) and some survival money, Herzog sets out from Munich on 23rd November and eventually arrives in Paris on 14th December. Along the way, he endures increasingly intense levels of physical discomfort, shelters from the hostile weather in chapels and farm buildings, breaks into unoccupied houses to sleep and gradually withdraws and tries to avoid any prospect of human contact:

Then snow, snow, rainy snow, snowy rain; I curse Creation. What for? I'm so utterly soaked that I avoid people by crossing sodden meadows, in order to save myself from facing them.

Rain, rain, rain, rain, rain, only rain, I can't recall anything more. It's become a steady, even drizzle and the roads become endless.

The soles burn from the red-hot core in the earth's interior.

In spite of all the physical ailments that Herzog endures, I find the book strangely uplifting as it is clear that the process of walking is an almost shamanic ritual that allows access to what he has described, in other interviews, as 'ecstatic truth'. It is as if the repeated act of placing one foot after another gradually opens up the mind to a transcendent dream state where fact and fiction merge and new ideas are born:

Traveling on foot has nothing to do with exercise. I spoke earlier about daydreaming and that I do not dream at nights. Yet when I am walking I fall deep into dreams. I float through fantasies and find myself inside unbelievable stories. I literally walk through whole novels and films, and football matches. I do not even look at where I am stepping, but I never lose my direction.

It is not difficult to imagine how Herzog's obsessive, driven characters may have been dreamt into being during this process of walking pilgrimage.

In *Wanderlust*, Rebecca Solnit makes the point that by going on a pilgrimage, one has left behind the complications of one's place in the world – family, hierarchy, and duty and the pilgrim enters a truly liminal state. A state of being-in-the-world on the cusp of past and future personal identity - a state of possibility. Solnit also reminds us that liminality is derived from the Latin *limin*, a threshold. As the pilgrim steps over the line, symbolically and physically, s/he is stripped of status and authority, removed from a social structure, maintained and sanctioned by power and force, and levelled to a homogenous state of being with fellow pilgrims through discipline and ordeal.

However, if the sacred pilgrim is bound by a sense of comradeship and communion with fellow travellers, there is no such comfort for Herzog and nor is any sought.

Herzog's existential, shamanic, pilgrimage also reminds me of the great Franco-Scottish poet, essayist and geopoetician_Kenneth White whose work is also centred on walking as a means of 'opening a world' and, in particular, establishing a fundamental relationship with planet

Earth. White was involved with Alexander Trocchi's Project Sigma in the 1960s and took part in the Paris *évenements* of 1968. This lost him his university teaching post which led to him going 'on a long walk in the Basque Country'. White is inspired by what he calls 'intellectual nomads' such as Friedrich Nietzsche, Arthur Rimbaud, Henry Thoreau and Patrick Geddes (all keen walkers) who he views as having wandered from the 'motorway of Western civilisation' in order to find new ways of thinking and living. (As an aside Giles Deleuze was one of the panel who judged White's doctoral thesis on intellectual nomadism). White has undertaken numerous long walks and geopoetic pilgrimages such as his travels in Asia which are collected in the volume *Pilgrim of the Void* (the title says it all!). This includes an account of White walking in the footsteps of Basho from Tokyo to Hokkaido:

All alone
with an old crow
in unfamiliar country

which reminds me of one of the rare occasions in Herzog's book where he achieves some form of solace and communion with the natural world:

A nuthatch was tapping on a tree and I stood there a while, listening to him, as it soothed me.

Off course, as Herzog arrives in Paris, the question has to be asked. What happened to Lotte Eisner? She is tired and weak, but still alive and given that she manages to push a chair over to Herzog, is possibly in better shape than he is:

Someone must have told her on the phone that I had come on foot – I didn't want to mention it. I was embarrassed and placed my smarting legs up on a second armchair which she pushed over to me. In the embarrassment a thought passed through my head and, since the situation was strange anyway, I told it to her. Together, I said, we shall boil fire and stop fish. Then she looked at me and smiled very delicately, and since she knew that I was someone on foot and therefore unprotected, she understood me. For one splendid, fleeting moment, something mellow flowed through my deadly tired body. I said to her, "Open the window. From these last days onward, I can fly."

Lotte Eisner lived for another nine years and died in 1983.

Now Playing: Thomas Köner – *Permafrost*

29th March 2012

References:

Paul Cronin, ed, (2003), *Herzog on Herzog*, (London, Faber & Faber).

Werner Herzog, (1978), *Of Walking in Ice,* (Delf, Free Association, English translation 2008).

Michael Gardiner, (2006), *From Trocchi to Trainspotting, Scottish Critical Theory since 1960* (Edinburgh, Edinburgh University Press).

Rebecca Solnit, (2001) *Wanderlust: A History of Walking* (London, Verso).

Kenneth White, (1992), *Pilgrim of the Void* (Edinburgh, Mainstream).

Observation on Weather and City Space

Slightly incongruous to be re-reading Werner Herzog's *Of Walking in Ice* whilst we all wallow in the sunshine this week. A bit like walking around with an ice-cube in my pocket as Edinburgh metamorphoses into an outdoor theatre and city life explodes on to the streets. It's interesting to think about how a hot snap of unseasonal weather can challenge the notion of city design, public space, and its usage. Groups and individuals start to congregate freely in the most unlikely of spaces under 'normal, seasonal, weather conditions'. The usual wet and windy expanse of the Usher Hall steps are transformed into a natural amphitheatre, for meeting, eating, drinking, thinking and reading. Any available sun-facing surface is colonised by the intrepid light worshipper including window sills and ledges. People appear to embrace drifting and strolling in their lunch hours, glad to be moving though the city with no particular purpose. I haven't really given too much thought about the relationship between weather and city space but when you see such an instant and radical transformation it is hard to ignore.

Now playing: Untitled - Birchville Cat Motel. Bruce Russell.

29th March 2012

Last Light

Conducting the last light of 2014

≈

Now playing: Keiji Haino/Jim O'Rourke/Oren Ambarchi - 'A New Radiance Springing Forth From Inside The Light' from *Now While It's Still Warm Let Us Pour In All The Mystery*.

31st December 2014

Resume, Resume

Staggering, blinking into radiant sunlight.

Fresh blossom, spring air,

salt tang, mirror sea.

Out here again,

move.

Out there again.

Resume,

Resume.

Now playing: Olivier Messiaen - *Catalogue d'Oiseaux*

30th April 2011

A-Field Further (with assorted Rag-Pickings)

The Firebugs of Kreuzberg

*Retain your memories
but détourn them
so that they correspond with your era.*

Asger Jorn

We are in Berlin travelling on the U-Bahn to Kottbusser Tor in Kreuzberg. It is a gloriously warm April morning with fists of sunlight starting to punch through the clouds. From the elevated train tracks we can survey the sweeping spread of the city below. In the foreground, a graffiti inscribed, cubist assemblage written on to the earth. "How do they manage to get up there to paint it?" asks R, pointing to a 3-D effect *trompe l'oeil* covering the entire gable end of a tall building. A and I marvel at the scale and ambition. An exploding riot of colour and illusion. We both shrug our shoulders...

I had been in Kreuzberg the previous evening at a gig in the HAU 2 theatre complex. (As an aside, I was delighted to discover later that this building was the original site of the Zodiak Free Arts Lab formed by Conrad Schnitzler, Hans-Joachim Roedelius and Boris Schaak in 1968. More on this below if interested. (1)). I didn't have much time to stroll around the streets beforehand but picked up a little of the night ambience. Clearly the zest to inscribe almost any available surface with graffiti and street art was alive and well. I realised that my previous visit to Berlin had been when the Wall was still standing and Kreuzberg was the beating heart of a chaotic, edgy, alternative radicalism. An enclave of squatters, artists and musicians, living cheek by jowl with the, largely Turkish, immigrant population. At the time it felt like some bunkered interzone within the island of Berlin. A city trapped and adrift in topography, history and cold war paranoia. Inter-railing around Europe, I remember having to scrape up the Deutschmarks to buy a ticket and visa to allow travel through the DDR from Hamburg. Walking out of Zoo Station with a head full of Berlin tropes: Bowie, Iggy, Lou Reed and *Christiane F.* I could imagine witnessing scenes of Blixa Bargeld and Nick Cave holding court in the bars of SO36 underneath the watch towers. On reflection, a romanticised, pop-culture depiction of the city shaped more by the *NME* than by any history or guide-book.

Around twenty-five years later I'm walking out of Kottbusser Tor station with the family still carrying these ghosts of memory. It feels a bit surreal to experience the bright sunshine and languid air of the street as we set off in search of the Turkish market down on the banks of the Landwehrkanal. We pass the grocery stores and a few cafes where groups of men (and it is all men) are sitting outside sipping Turkish coffee and gossiping. It's only a short walk to the canal and it evidently becomes apparent that we have either got the day or our directions wrong. There is no sign of any Turkish market. Perhaps Bowie, Iggy and Blixa can help guide us? Feed us a few signs? However, R is already off. A nine-year old is not going to hang around whilst our putative tour guides attempt to get their shit together.

♦

Unburdened by worldly cares, unfettered by learning, free of ingrained habit, negligent of time, the child is open to the world.

Yi-Fu Tuan

Children are natural and consummate psychogeographers. They can happily drift through any environment, urban or rural, seeking out and following the signs of place that speak to them. With the city as potential playground R, starts to saunter on ahead of us, leading the drift, although, of course, not aware or caring that this is what is happening. We wander along the tree-lined canal path for a good stretch and apart from the dog shit, and occasional jogger, the city takes on an almost rural feel. Bowie, Iggy and Blixa are struggling to keep up. I think they may have stopped for a fag. The sunlight is clearly not agreeing with them.

I could feel the interest of our spectral trio dissolve even further as we sat down on a bench to marvel at two magnificent white swans and a group of mallards bobbing on the canal. "How do the swans keep so white in the city?" A pleasure boat chugs past and the gentle wake lip-lips against the canal sides. Our quiet reverie is broken when the larger swan rises out of the water, and extends its full wingspan. For a moment it looks as if the wingtips will almost touch either side of the canal. A few strong beats and the swan takes to the air. We wonder where it can be heading and whether the birds flew freely between East and West when the Wall was up.

Against a riot of cubist, Kreuzberg colour
- *"Fuck Yuppies - Reclaim the Streets"*
a white swan rises from the water
outstretched wings unfurling
almost, pushing
the canal walls apart.

We can feel ourselves being pulled into another city world as a ladybird lands on A's arm. I love how ladybirds always look hand painted. After watching it run over her skin, it pauses to open its tiny wings as if basking in the sun. R lets it run on to her fingers and kneels down to reunite the hand daubed, smudge of colour with the greenery beneath the lime trees. She discovers the bustling activities of an ant colony and we observe the industry of the leaf carrying comrades, marching in their regimented lines - lugging, organising, creating. Sucked in closer to the unfolding drama of this animistic, micro world, we start to notice other flecks of red and black moving amongst the earthy shades of leaf mould. They are not ladybirds. We are looking at hordes of small insects that are completely unknown to us. Some scurry around alone, whilst others pile on top of each other to accumulate into little shuffling balls

  of red and black. Too absorbed in the moment, we 'forget' to take a picture of them. It is only once we are home that we eventually manage to find an image and identify these mysterious little creatures as firebugs. From now on they will be known as The Firebugs of Kreuzberg.

Time has dissolved as we eventually head away from the canal and start to re-enter Kreuzberg street life. We start to notice the hum of cars again. A Mad Max biker type walks past with a tiny dog on a pink lead. The dog is sporting a bandanna. Our drift takes us up the entire length of Oranienstrasse, the main street of the district. It is still pretty quiet in daylight and we pass the door of SO36, the club where Bowie and Iggy used to hang out and, by now, have probably once again, taken refuge. R has commandeered the camera and is now taking photographs, still drifting through a city more akin to Hayao Miyazaki's animistic universe than my one populated with spectral ghosts. The signs are speaking:

The Red Bulls of Oranienstrasse

The Goddess and Protector of Oranienstrasse

The Visitor (detail from the side of a parked van)

We eventually return full circle and ascend the steps back up to Kottbusser Tor station. Our quest to find Turkish markets, and gain enlightenment from Bowie, Iggy and Blixa has failed. They have all remained spectral and elusive. Our drift has pulled us into another dimension of Kreuzberg. One of canal paths, white swans, mallards, ants, and red bulls. Above all, we have discovered and witnessed something mysterious and new. The red and black insects that we now know as The Firebugs of Kreuzberg.

Now playing: Kluster – *Klopfzeichen*

30th June 2013

♦ ♦

(1) HAU 2 and The Zodiak Free Arts Lab

I was excited to learn that, after a hiatus of twelve years, Keith Rowe, Oren Ambarchi, Christian Fennesz, Peter Rehberg (Pita) and Pimmon were reconvening their curiously named *Afternoon Tea* project for one night only in Kreuzberg. It was delightful happenstance to discover that this was happening on one of the nights of our holiday. I headed down to the HAU 2 venue and certainly wasn't disappointed. One long piece saw this stellar ensemble layer up a set of dark, fractured shards of glitch improv, punctuated with blankets of shimmering serenity. A deep, meditative, all embracing sound. An unfolding. Ambarchi sat almost motionless unleashing his trademark sonic 'depth charges'. The aural equivalent of watching and feeling a lava lamp. The bass resonance of the note entering through the feet and traveling up and out of the body. It was also good to see Keith Rowe having to play in a much louder and busier sound environment than the last couple of times I've encountered him. Fennesz couldn't help but attempt to excavate and instil some melodic fragments into the proceedings whilst Rehberg and Pimmon intervened with pincer movements of laptop noise assault. All in all a fabulous event to witness and experience in the dark, minimal space of HAU 2.

The happenstance of this event was further enhanced when I later discovered that HAU 2 was actually the original site of the Zodiak Free Arts Lab or Zodiac Club, formed by Conrad Schnitzler, Hans-Joachim Roedelius and Boris Schaak in 1968. Whilst only open for a few months, the Zodiak was a melting pot where "freaks and avant-gardists of all stripes could enjoy live psychedelia, free jazz, free performance and freakout". (A1). It was a space also directly responsible for the emergence of Kluster (Schnitzler/Roedelius/Moebius) and Tangerine Dream, at that time with Schnitzler and Klaus Schulz in the ranks. This early incarnation of the Tangs is light years away from the vapid new-age pap that they later embraced in the 1980s.

The first few Kluster albums were engineered by a young Conny Plank who brought his experience of working with Edgar Varese to give some shape and coherence to the brutalist improvised chaos of this embryonic kosmische music. With the subsequent exit of Schnitzler and a later name change to Cluster, the sound took on a softer edge and the recording of classic kosmische albums such as *Cluster II, Zuckerzeit, Sowiesoso and Cluster & Eno*. The Zodiak also hosted performances by, amongst others, Agitation Free, Ash Ra Tempel, Human Being, Peter Brotzmann and Alexander Von Schlippenbach.

I love it when buildings can reveal their embedded memories like this. From a few months activity, the ripples from the epicentre are still being felt.

(A1) Nikolaos Kotsopoulos (Ed), (2009), *Krautrock: Cosmic Rock and Its Legacy*, (London: black dog publishing).

Postscript: The (Other) Firebugs of Kreuzberg

© Tom Spree

A short postscript to *The Firebugs of Kreuzberg:*

A friend from Berlin commented that the piece was quite different from what they had anticipated from the title:

"You do know about the other Firebugs of Kreuzberg right?"

"Eh, no ... remember, it was only a fleeting visit whilst on holiday!"

I was helpfully sent a clutch of links to some newspaper articles which outline how 'firebug' arson attacks on high-end cars have been increasing in Berlin in recent years. It would appear that BMW, Mercedes and Porsche are the favoured brands to toast. There is a long history of traditional May Day protests in Kreuzberg culminating in car burnings, however, these articles suggest that the number of politically motivated firebug attacks is increasing. The attacks appear to be an expression of both anti-gentrification protest and also of a more general grievance against 'the rich' as Germany attempts to navigate the global, economic malaise. The record annual number of car burnings in Berlin was previously 401 in 2009. In April 2012, it was reported that this had risen to over 700 in 2011. Whilst car burning incidents have taken place across Berlin, the majority cluster around the central districts of Kreuzberg, Mitte and Prenzlauer Berg. Not surprisingly, these are places where the usual gentrification tensions arise between relatively wealthy incomers and poor long-term residents and play out against rising rents and property prices and the polarization of employment opportunities.

Trying to attribute arson attacks as politically motivated or copycat vandalism is not something that the politicians or police appear to wish to address although an unemployed man was jailed in April 2012 for seven years. He was prosecuted on 86 charges of arson involving 102 cars. As a motive he said that he: "hated the affluent". Meanwhile, given the sheer number of car burnings, it looks as if many other disaffected 'firebugs' continue to evade detection, regardless of motive.

As a final aside, I was also interested to receive a comment from Emina Redzic who recognised the insects in the original piece. In Serbia they are called "palikuce" or as directly translated into English "arsonists".

Perhaps these little insects may be even more mysterious than we originally thought.

Selected References:

1 . Berlin Police Chief: Don't Park Fancy Cars in Kreuzberg

2. Berlin's burning cars a hot topic in forthcoming elections

3. Arsonists Torch Berlin Porsches, BMWs on Economic Woe

4. Berlin as Battleground: "Don't Park your Porsche in Kreuzberg"

5. Arsonist Gets 7 Years for Burning Luxury Vehicles.

Now Playing: Swans - We Rose From Your Bed With The Sun In Our Head

9th August 2012

Newcastle upon Tyne: An Assemblage in 16 Fragments

I

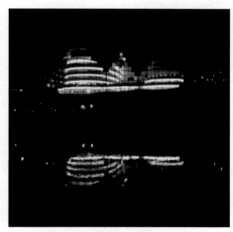

The Sage Gateshead at night

I remember

How the darkness doubled

Standing. In the dark, enveloped by a light rain on the quayside of the River Tyne. The opening lines of Television's *Marquee Moon* are snaking through my head. It feels as if the song is seeping out into the city's arteries. An energy circulating through the cobbled streets, overhead bridges and the reflecting river. *Marquee Moon* is an album that has always seemed to stand outside of time and yet evokes a strong sense of place. An almost cubist portrait of New York. Tonight it's Newcastle that is being pulled into the gravity of the song.

The treacly purr of the Tyne does indeed double the darkness upon which two cathedrals of light are painted. The Sage Gateshead, a silver slug of undulating movement in daylight, shape-shifts into a trio of glass pyramids. Bricks of light etched upon the darkness. Its reflective *doppelgänger* is traced in the depths of the lipping water. All edges smoothed into Guggenheim-esque spirals of shimmering curves.

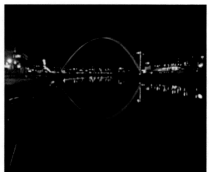

I recall

lightning struck itself

Further up the quayside, the Millenium Bridge indicates the route of travel over the river to where Tom Verlaine & Co will shortly take the stage for a very rare UK appearance. Once again the city appears to absorb and reflect back the enigmatic lyric. Lightning/lighting appearing to strike itself. An arc of rainbow colours - the illusion of movement a solid sphere - a *Marquee Moon*?

II

At the Hatton Gallery, Newcastle University:

Pasmore's description of the Apollo Pavillion as "an architecture and sculpture of purely abstract form through which to walk".

III

The Merzbarn Wall

I recall being alerted by Diana J. Hale to Kurt Schwitter's Merzbarn near Elterwater in the Lake District. Created in 1947 - 48 the Merzbarn was Kurt Schwitters' final, and in his own estimation, 'greatest', piece of work.

The Hatton Gallery has on display, as a permanent installation, the Merzbarn Wall which was part of the original barn construction at Elterwater. The Wall was unfinished when Schwitters died in 1948 and in 1965, after lengthy discussions about the barn's future, the Wall was given to Newcastle University who undertook its removal, restoration and preservation. The Merzbarn was based on Schwitter's idea of collage, in which found items are incorporated into an art work. Schwitters applied a rough layer of decorator's plaster and painted over various found objects, giving the three-dimensional collage an abstract quality. The items incorporated into the wall include:

A slate log splitter
A small metal window frame
The rose of a child's watering can
Twigs
Part of the rim of a cartwheel
A china egg
A section of guttering
Part of an oval gold mirror frame
A metal grid
A rubber ball
Stones from Langdale Beck
Some Gentians – which have now disappeared

Asked what the Merzbarn Wall meant, Schwitters replied: "all it is, is form and colour, just form and colour".

The Merz Barn, 1947 (Postcard)

Schwitters on his 60th Birthday, 20th June 1947 (Postcard)

Merzbau - the creation of environments which use the forms and even debris from local places to create a new environment. Initially in the form of assemblages, Schwitters developed the human scale environments which he called *Merzbau*.

The Merzbarn Wall, Hatton
Gallery Newcastle

The Merzbarn Wall - Detail I

IV

Kittiwakes on the Tyne

© Darrell Birkett

From March until August, Newcastle/Gateshead quayside becomes home to around 600 pairs of breeding Kittiwakes. Normally found on coastal cliffs, the Tyne Kittiwakes clearly prefer the narrow ledges of the Tyne bridges. The Kittiwake colony is the furthest inland anywhere in the world and makes Newcastle one of the few cities to have a seabird colony in its centre.

There are no Kittiwakes to be observed on this visit as they will be out soaring on Atlantic winds over the winter. Some will travel as far as Canada and Greenland. However, it is comforting to know that come Spring, they will once again hear the unheard pulse of the city guiding them back to their breeding grounds on the bridges of the Tyne.

V

The Bigg Market

A lonely carved stone huddles unceremoniously in the Bigg market. The elegance and grace of the craftsmanship still evident and contrasted against the utilitarian tardis of the neighbouring, municipal rubbish bin. The stone, in its displaced environment, is now likely to be a seated sanctuary for the nocturnal fag smokers taking a breather from *Club Luna* next door. A silent witness to the human stains from last nights excess dried hard against the pavement.

VI

A steampunk kind of city. A collision of multi-level curves and cobbles as retro-futuristic bridges cut across the sky.

VII

Saturday at 12.15pm

Under a shifting sky

a chorus of angels

         - of the North

sing to the wind.

Cathedral bells

flood the city

sound spilling

around

Amen Corner.

VIII

 Powered by steam: the tendrils that connect the local into webs of possibilities and extended horizons. Encounters with the other. Creating an expansive map.

IX

The curious case of the virtual building at Trinity Chare on 57 Quayside. Did this building once exist here? It would appear improbable.

Explore behind the facade of the spectacle:

Behind the Virtual

X

Herbs in the City

Broad Garth

Botany scrutinised at the bottom of walls

asphalt's rust

imaginable palpation raises them to the dignity of

plants

emanated from the earth

to the condition of contention

                              - Raymond Queneau - from *Hitting the Streets*

XI

"Dare to be Free"

XII

Turning from the river, the narrow vennel (chare?) of Watergate frames Bessie Surtees House. All wobbly frames of black and white like a hand drawn illustration. This was the scene on 18th December 1772 when a

young, 17-year-old Bessie, daughter of a rich banker, climbed out of a window to elope with her lover to Scotland. It was considered such a major scandal at the time that people would come to stand and stare at the house.

I stand and stare at the house before learning of this story.

XIII

A shift of level. With a final look back to the river, a chinese box of stairwells unfold to lead up towards the (New) Castle Keep and the Black Gate.

Looking back to the river

So he resumed his walk, but the way proved long. For the street he was in ... did not lead up to the Castle hill, it only made towards it and then, as if deliberately, turned aside, and though it did not lead away from the Castle it got no nearer to it either.

Franz Kafka *The Castle*

XIV

A very well-preserved ghost sign built into the brickwork. It can always be seen on any train journey that passes through Newcastle.

The building is a rare surviving witness to the replacement of the horse by the motor car. Originally built in 1897 as a horse, carriage and cycle auction room it was essentially a showroom for horse-drawn carriages. By the 1920s the future prospects of horse-drawn transport were pretty bleak so the building was adapted to serve as one of the first motor car garages and dealerships. I subsequently find out that the building stands on top of, part of the buried remains, of Hadrian's Wall.

Layered histories converse in the topography of place.

XV

A fixed departure train ticket means that time is running short so no time to look for a building that I have heard so much about: The Literary and Philosophical Society of Newcastle Upon Tyne or The Lit & Phil as it appears to be known locally. Serendipity intervenes and I stumble across the building very close to the station only to discover a one day book sale in progress. Twenty minutes to browse before the train leaves. I trust the space and know that the books will call out. They do. It all works and it's a short walk to the station to catch the train.

XVI

As the train heads northwards, I nod to Coopers Motor Mart. No longer simply a sign from a train window but time stacked in layers as a material place which the act of walking has 'made real'.

A trace of footsteps are left behind. One more scratch upon the city streets and a drift through one version of Newcastle is assembled in memory. A small fragment of fragments. The city, carried within.

≈

Merzbau - the creation of environments which use the forms and even debris from local places to create a new environment.

≈

Now Playing: Tom Verlaine - *Warm and Cool*

4th February 2013

References

The Apollo Pavillion

The Hatton Gallery, University of Newcastle.

Kurt Schwitters and the Merzbarn Wall

The Wall, the harsh building of the Merzbarn

(Always) Between Something and Nothing

The white centre ... is both an emptiness and an energy generator. Your eye is continually drawn back to its white silence, its void-ness. Then your attention is propelled out again along the twisting road-ways. The eye cycles back and forth between "something" and "nothing".

First Rauschenberg laid down a base coat of white paint on a 48-by-32 inch piece of masonite. Then on the top four-fifths of this white ground, he pasted pieces of maps of American cities: Minneapolis, Pittsburgh, St Louis, New Orleans Boston, Denver...

The twisting spidery roadways - dark lines radiating across off-white backgrounds crackle with shivery linear energy. This frenetic activity is silenced at the pictures centre by a great white circular void that hovers like a pulsating energy field. This void isn't empty. Literally it's a layer of brushed white paint that laps over the cut edges of the maps. Visually, the painted surface dematerialises into a humming whiteness.

Kay Larson on Robert Rauschenberg's *Mother of God*

I recently finished Kay Larson's wonderful book *Where the Heart Beats: John Cage, Zen Buddhism and the Inner Life of Artists*. I don't particularly want to offer a review here but if you have any interest in John Cage then I guess that you will be well rewarded by reading it.

Like any great book, it's the ideas that linger around afterwards that are of greatest value. They push prod and poke. Unconscious spectres haunting the edges of conscious thought before demanding some form of engagement, application or reflection. This perhaps explains why, for a few minutes last weekend I stood, in the dark, on a motorway bridge at Charing Cross, Glasgow. A walk back to the station interrupted by thoughts about "something" and "nothing". The traffic of the M8 motorway cascading underneath my feet and I'm recording it on my phone...

Well clearly my silent piece...expresses the acceptance of whatever happens in that emptiness. And the same thing was expressed by that empty painting, that white painting of Bob Rauschenberg.

John Cage

One of the most fascinating parts of Larson's book deals with Cage's conceptual evolution leading up to his (in)famous 'silent' piece *4'33"*. Larson makes the case that prior to *4'33"*, Cage's thinking was expressed in Either / Or dualities. His two lectures: *Lecture on Something* and *Lecture on Nothing* bookend this approach. Increasingly inspired by the Zen lectures of D. T. Suzuki at Columbia University and the white paintings of Robert Rauschenberg, Cage moved towards the idea of the radical act that was required to detonate these dualisms. His famous visit to the anechoic (sound-proof) chamber at Harvard had shown Cage that 'silence' could never be an absolute absence of sound. Even in the scientifically quietest place on Earth he could still hear sounds. The high whine of his own nervous system and dull roar of his blood circulation. He heard the sound of his life in process and Cage concluded that there is no such thing as silence.

Silence is not acoustic. It is a change of mind, a turning around.

4'33" embodies the idea of life and art as a *process*. As Larson says: "before anything else, it's an experience." It is a proposition that says, in notational shorthand: stop for a moment and look around you and listen; stop and look; stop and listen. "Something" and "Nothing" can never be divided.

Well I use it (4'33") constantly in my life experience. No day goes by without my making use of that piece in my life and in my work...I turn my attention towards it. I realize that it's going on continuously...

This may all sound pretty abstract but two events from a recent afternoon wander through Glasgow bring it all home. Heading back from the West End, the energetic bustle of Byers Road noticeably slips off the shoulders as you enter Kelvingrove Park. Welcomed into the crisp and brittle air by the bare winter trees, very few people are around and circumstances are conspiring to shift towards something approaching an urban 'silence'. (The ubiquitous, low hum of traffic is always there, much like the sound of Cage's blood circulation). Slipping into a kind of unconscious walking reverie, measured out in the rhythm of movement, I was brought completely into the moment by the spooling song of possibly a mistle thrush or song thrush high in a tree. What an enchanting experience to simply stop and listen to the cadences and Fi-ga-ro Fi-ga-ro refrains weaving a thread of song through the urban silence. An oscillation between something and nothing. Lives in process. I managed to capture around 40 seconds on a pretty rough phone recording, by which time several people had gathered around wondering what I was looking at:

.

.

[sometimelater]

.

.

309

I wanted to be quiet in a nonquiet situation.

Later in the early evening, it is already dark and I'm walking back into the town centre. I stop on the motorway flyover bridge at Charing Cross. For a short time I just watch the traffic swoosh past underneath. Pools of light flooding the motorway and dispersing within seconds. The experience is strangely mesmerising and calming. The rhythms of sound vary depending on the sequence and number of cars across the three lanes. Like a childhood game, I start to guess which lane a car will appear in next. A chance operation in process. I then notice that occasionally there can be an almost complete drop out towards a momentary void of sound. For a few seconds no cars are in view in any of the lanes.

After a few minutes of this hypnotic experience, I realise that I've been in the white centre of Rauschenberg's painting. The void. Quiet in a nonquiet situation. As I lift my head to look around, the roads and paths of the city spiral off in every direction. Energies of neon, arteries of possibility, encounters, histories and stories yet to come.

I walk towards Sauchiehall Street, always poised between something and nothing.

Now playing: Kevin Drumm – *Tannenbaum*

10th February 2013

References:

Richard Konstelanetz (ed), *Conversing with Cage* (London: Omnibus Press, 1989).

Kay Larson, *Where the Heart Beats: John Cage, Zen Buddhism and the Inner Life of Artists,* (New York: The Penguin Press. 2012).

Robert Rauschenberg, *Mother of God*, 1950. San Francisco Museum of Modern Art.

Special thanks to Fraser Macdonald and Louise Arber for offering suggestions as to the identity of the singing bird. The wonder of Twitter.

A Short Visual Drift through the Edinburgh New Town

Pedagogy

~

Converge/Entwine

~

Broughton Market with rainbow

~

The Old/The New

~

Broughton Street with smudge of moon

~

Urban Fox

~

Now Playing: Barbara Monk Feldman - *The Northern Shore*
15th May 2013

This Land ...

◇

This land

these   rocks and stones

vessels of deep time

being   before

being inscribed

in landscape

before   being

named and claimed

as landscape.

This land

a made place

a place   made

to build, dwell

be settled.

Gone now

gone.   Only

ghosts and bocans

sounding

the stones   over

peat bog, moss

moor and lichen.

.

Breathe and feel

the chiliastic serenity

of this uncanny land.

◇

I rediscovered this photograph recently which was taken a couple of years ago at Machrie Moor on the Isle of Arran. We were on holiday and I went out at around 6.00am to go for a walk before the family were up. It's about 2.5km to the stones from the closest road, which is long enough to immerse yourself in the feeling of the place. The photograph is of the main grouping of stones which stand amongst a ritual landscape consisting of seven stone circles, several chambered cairns and hut circles. A highly evocative liminal landscape to wander alone in the thin morning light wrapped in light drizzle. Whilst written at a different time of the day, I cannot better the feeling described by John McArthur in *The Antiquities of Arran* (1861):

We have never witnessed a wilder and more grandly solemn scene than these old circles on the Mauchrie Moor, looming in shadowy indistinctiveness of an autumn moonlight...as we wandered amongst the old ruins, the weirdly stirring legends of the past haunted our mind, til the wreaths of mist seemed to float about like shadowy phantoms and the circling monoliths and hoary cromlech appeared to rise from the heath, like ghosts of the heroes of old, bending around the grave of their buried chief.

On my way back to the road, I'm reflecting on the tales of local folklore and particularly the stories of the bocans (malign spirits) which are said to inhabit the area. I'm rolling some sheep trintle in my hand - those soft wisps of wool which get snagged on fences or whin. It was as quiet as a remote landscape could be. Only the occasional bird call, a tuft of wind, the soft fizz of drizzle. Amongst all the greens and browns, I'm distracted by an impressive growth of witches butter, that bright yellow, almost golden fungus and head over for a closer look. I'm just about to step over a large tuft of moor grass, when, as is their wont, a pheasant takes wing from almost underneath my foot, squawking like a banshee. As the bird ascends in that awkward, unbalanced, flapping squall a tail feather whirligigs down from the sky which I manage to catch just before it hits the ground.

A gift from the moor dwellers to soothe my pounding heart.

Pheasant Feather/Sheep Trintle Cloud

Now playing: Eliane Radigue - Koumé, the third part of *Trilogie de la Mort*.

24th May 2012

Bouncing on Sacrilege: Deller, Debord and Jumping for Joy

It is futile to search in our theories of architecture or dérive for any other motive than the passion for play.

Guy Debord (1)

As we enter Glasgow Green, my daughter takes aim, like an archer pulling a bowstring and points to the horizon. "There it is!" We both follow the trajectory of the imaginary arrow and gaze over the vast expanse of green common land. From all directions, ant-like threads of people are drifting towards the iconic structure of Stonehenge sitting in the landscape. The lines of people are converging and congregating around the monument and we can hear the distant sounds of carnival. Feeling the totemic pull of the stones, we set off to join them. This is why we have come.

Except this Stonehenge is Jeremy Deller's ultimate bouncy castle version. An interactive art installation named *Sacrilege* and part of the Glasgow International Festival of Visual Art. Such is the popularity of *Sacrilege*, that, on arrival, we are assigned to one of the two holding 'pens' which allow up to one hundred people, at a time, to assemble and wait for a fifteen minute 'interactive experience' with the exhibit. As we sit in the sunshine, and soak up the celebration taking place amongst the stones, it really is a joy to watch the utter delight on faces as they attempt to run, jump, roll, lie or simply walk. Toddlers are happy to bounce up and down on the spot whilst the older kids are going off like pressure cookers, doing cartwheels, forward rolls, playing tig and body slamming into the iconic henge. Adults are given licence to do pretty much the same if they can keep up. A tribe of teenage goths stick to the perimeter, appearing to be disoriented by the brilliant sunshine and riot of lurid green plastic. Some pilgrims simply take refuge at the base of a stone and observe.

What also contributes to the *Sacrilege* experience is how the area is completely cleared between pen changeovers. For a short period of time the empty installation is replete with possibility, creating a sense of playful anticipation in the crowd as shoes are kicked off, jerseys discarded and bags are heaped in piles. The good-humoured security crew attempt to enforce their mock authority as they patrol the 'control zone' between crowd and structure, yakking into their walkie talkies. An anarchic youngster unable to contain herself, sneaks under the rope and makes a dash for the centre before being retrieved, kicking and screaming, by a slightly embarrassed parent. The heid bummer security guard with the megaphone barks out instructions ("no shoes, heavy bags, human sacrifice") and the rope is finally dropped with all the ceremony of an Olympic starting gun. It's a mad, mad rammy to clamber on to the structure and within seconds all ontological baggage is released by the sheer thrill of being and bouncing in the moment. When our turn comes around we (I!) soon find that fifteen minutes of plastic stone hi-jinks is pretty exhausting but exhilarating. We are part of a communal assemblage, literally jumping for joy. Sacrilege indeed.

I'm not overly familiar with Deller's work, but afterwards it struck me that there is a lot more going on with this bouncy castle than at first may appear. I'm reminded of Ralph Rumney and Guy Debord's attraction to the *ludic* ideas of Huizinga who proposed that spontaneity, play and festival should be a vital part of daily life and a potentially transformative agent to break free from the 'stultifying nature of boring, non-ludic life'. Hussey suggests that Huizinga's arguments had a revolutionary significance for Debord who was intrigued by the suggestion that games or spontaneous play could be experimental forms of new social behaviour. Rumney claims to have introduced Huizinga's *Homo Ludens* to Debord which was instrumental in providing him with a vocabulary for thinking about and anticipating 'the construction of situations'. If nothing else, Deller has certainly constructed a situation. I'm also reminded of Bakhtin's notion of the carnivalesque whereby the participation in carnival can remove individuals from the social hierarchies of everyday non-carnival life and allow the exercise of normally repressed energies to flower. Perhaps *Sacrilege* can be viewed as a practice of Situationist détournement. By hi-jacking the iconic image of Stonehenge, and all of its associated cultural baggage, Deller has created a new artwork that celebrates free assembly, mass appeal and the carnivalesque. Perhaps more importantly it is playful, fun, cheeky and joyous. Not terms that would leap to mind should you visit the original Wiltshire version. I understand that *Sacrilege* is now heading to 'the Olympics' and it will be interesting to observe whether the Glasgow experience will be 'allowed' to translate to a very different cultural space. Will anyone be able to pitch up at will, freely assemble and take part? We shall observe with interest.

And as we join the dehydrated but elated crowd drifting over the green common land to the winter gardens of the People's Palace, we also take the chance to view the people's history of Glasgow. A history of grim social conditions and top-down imposed planning failures, leavened with histories of resistance. My daughter is particularly taken with two iconic artefacts from popular culture: Billy Connolly's banana boots and Alex

Harvey's leather jacket. Two performers, who also know/knew something about invoking the carnivalesque.

So here we are, with freedom
within our sweaty, greedy, grasps.
So remember this, boys and girls,
when freedom comes along...
DON'T pish in the water supply...

Alex Harvey

Now playing: The Sensational Alex Harvey Band – *Live*

5th May 2012

References:

(1) Guy Debord, 'Architecture and Play' *Potlach* no. 20 (May 30, 1955).

(2) Andrew Hussey, (2001), *The Game of War: The Life and Death of Guy Debord* (London, Jonathan Cape).

Berlin Dérive – Tiergarten

Not to find one's way around a city does not mean much. But to lose one's way in a city, as one loses one's way in a forest, requires some schooling.

Walter Benjamin

awaken,
to the spooling thread
of a blackbird's raga
gravity loosens and
Berlin floats - just a little

just off the Ku'damm
a corporate glass palace
with outdoor aviary
squawks and fireworks of
green and red, caged
and displayed as trophies.

did the birds
of East and West
sing different songs?
can walls ever
constrain the birds?

that moment when
subterranean shackles
are shattered and

the S-Bahn explodes
into light.

drifting back from
the *bauhaus-archiv*
having just read
of the stormtroopers
arriving on 11th April 1933

the bauhaus is closed
but minds and ideas
continue to expand

I

In the old hunting forest
under the gaze of
the golden angel
quiet stillness
mute graffiti bunker

I could be the last
person on earth

II

footprints in
the children's sandbox
a trace of presence
a presence of absence

III

the open-air museum
of street lamps

a chronology of gas
technology and progress

a timeline

illuminating a history
of human darkness.

IV

her skull shattered
and a bullet in the head
Rosa sinks under
the dark water of the
Landwehr canal
her flickering flame
snuffed out

distant sparks kindle...

V

blue stars are pushing through
but today huddle for warmth

blackbirds, finches,
and a leering zoo
hyena for company.

Now playing: Einstürzende Neubauten - Strategies Against Architecture III (1991
- 2001)

25th April 2012

Whilst Looking for Somewhere Else

The future is already haunting us

(whilst looking for the Anne Frank Huis, Amsterdam)

Cubist dreams

of glass and sky

in-worlds

bleed

out-world

few bicycles

no canals

(lost somewhere between Amsterdam and Amstelveen looking for
the CoBrA museum)

≈

in Amstelveen, still looking for the CoBrA museum

≈

Now Playing: Getachew Mekuria & The Ex & Friends - *Y'Anbessaw Tezeta*
4th May 2014

An Encounter with the Uncanny

And we

       who always think

           of happiness *rising*

would feel the emotion

       that almost startles us

           when a happy thing *falls*.

Rainer Maria Rilke - *Duino Elegies*

≈

It often happens. A sensation at the edge of perception. A glint of light, a fluttering of movement. The feeling that some-thing has flitted across the threshold of the senses.

Something there - but not there.

And so it was, walking along the tree-lined footpath by St Mary's Cathedral in Edinburgh. Looking up, amongst the trees it was difficult to see it clearly at first. Something metallic, floating, but also appearing to be entwined amongst the branches, merged with the sky. It was only when a light breeze, initiated a gentle rocking movement that the suspended human form fully emerged.

From another angle, the drifting figure resembled a pencil drawing sketched on to the sky. A shaded human form floating against the blue canvas, slowly dissolving back into leaf and branch.

The gentle motion, both hypnotic and dreamlike conjured up thoughts of Solveig Dommartin's character, Marion, in Wim Wenders' *Wings of Desire*. A lonely trapeze artist, inhabiting the space between ground and sky, who entices an angel down to Earth.

I have subsequently read other people describe the St Mary's work as "sinister, creepy or disturbing" and it certainly startles you when you first look up and see it. An experience that I'm sure would be intensified if you encountered it in the dark under moonlight. However, for me, the figure conjured up a sensation of something otherworldly, yet strangely familiar. A fluid form of substance and air, swinging silently, and like 'Marion' suspended between the earth and sky.

From a distance I watched for a short time as many people passed along the footpath. The vast majority did not look up or see the figure suspended amongst the leaves. Silently watching, waiting to transform the everyday city into an encounter with the uncanny.

≈

Now playing: Nick Cave and the Bad Seeds - *The Carny*

22nd May 2014

I have found out that the sculpture is a work called *Spirit* by Aliisa Hyslop, a Finnish/Scottish artist. *Spirit* is presently part of an exhibition at the Arusha Art Gallery.

The quotation from Rilke's *Duino Elegies* are the last lines of the translation by David Young (New York: W.W. Norton & Company, 1978). Wim Wenders cites *Duino Elegies* as the initial inspiration for *Wings of Desire*.

A Haunting of Leaves

≈

there - not there
an x-ray of silence
a haunting of leaves

≈

≈

lumen etched

filigree of shadowplay

fading flux of

earth   root   breath

a fragile grounding

a passing cloud

here - not here

≈

From a walk in Wester Shore Woods, near Blackness Castle, south shore of the Firth of Forth.

Now playing: Jakob Ullmann - disappearing musics

14th August 2013

Dead Cars Dream ...

```
                    c

        d    e    a    d

        r         r

        e         s

        a

        m
```

```
                                    c
                    d       e       a       d
                                    r

                                    s

                                    d

                                    r

                                    e

                    a   l   c   h   e   m   y

                    m
```

Now playing: Poltergeist- Your Mind is a Box (Let Us Fill It With Wonder).
Photographs taken in Digbeth, Birmingham.
22nd July 2013

La Pasionaria and the Psychedelic Tiger: A short wander in Glasgow

Watch a street and you become it. You construct, if so inclined, a narrative: but you are also part of the witnessed event. You shape what you see.

Iain Sinclair, *Edge of the Orison*

In Glasgow. Uncharacteristic, sweltering heat and a half hour to spare before the gig. Just enough time for a quick wander, to stretch the legs without expectation. A phone camera will have to suffice if anything should reveal itself.

Out of the Arches, underneath Central Station, and into air larded with deep-fried food aromas and traffic fumes. I'm scanning for a sign to get started. Pastel shades shout out for attention and it seems that even the graffiti is responding to the sunshine:

Can't help noticing the little green archipelago thriving around the base. The resilience of nature to establish existence, in the most barren of conditions, at a busy city centre intersection.

Head down towards the river and pick up the trail:

More dancing colour to puncture the grey. A Bernard Edwards bass line bounces around in the head.

Walk straight on for a bit and over to the right there is a figure, facing towards the river, which looks interesting. From the rear I'm assuming it's some form of religious icon, arms stretched out to heaven? St Mungo perhaps? Cross the road and down a shallow incline of steps to view the figure face on.

A bunch of flowers. Wilting in the heat is tucked into the base of the statue. Obviously, still an active site of memory and remembrance. The plaque directly underneath the figure reads:

BETTER TO DIE ON YOUR FEET THAN LIVE FOR EVER ON YOUR KNEES — Dolores Ibarruri (La Pasionaria)

The statue is of Dolores Ibárruri (1895-1989), "La Pasionaria" ("The Passion Flower"), a heroine and leader in the Spanish Republican and Communist movements. An inspiration to the volunteers of the International Brigade who fought in the Spanish Civil War of 1936-1939.

I subsequently find out the sculpture is by Liverpool artist Arthur Dooley, who created the famous Beatles statue, *Four Lads Who Shook the World*. I was even more shocked to learn that Dooley never saw *La Pasionaria* installed, unable to afford the bus fare to come to Glasgow.

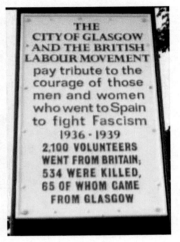

Continuing along the riverside walkway, a few people are taking full advantage of the heat wave. "Taps aff". Sitting, lying down, starfished, enjoying being out-of-doors, heads raised, eyes closed, embracing the setting sun. A sense of the more usual activities of the area are perhaps revealed as a young man is pulled up by two patrolling police officers and asked to empty his pockets.

Underneath another bridge to come face-to-face with a psychedelic tiger. A fiery flux of shifting colours, crouched and ready to pounce on the indolent walker:

Ascending from the river up a miniature Odessa Steps, I half expect a pram to come toppling over the top.

...and I'm facing Morrison's Bar which looks like it may never have opened since Jim checked out:

Around the corner, The Riverside Club doesn't look to be doing much business either. Perhaps these are 'badger' venues - they only come out in the dark?

I head into what I find is Fox Street. Looking back towards the east, the setting sun fracturing into shards hitting the ecclesiastical windows of a distant church:

Continuing west will take me back towards the City Centre:

Past the silent runners:

and the ghosts of Christmas Past:

and what could be a detail from the Boyle Family's *Journey to the Surface of the Earth* project:

Along with the heat and the sunshine, two cheerful lovehearts brighten up the street:

And a message a few feet away. No addressee. No object of affection. No initials. Just a statement addressed to whom?

I walk up towards Renfield Lane, thinking about how even the shortest of walks through a city can surprise, enchant and provoke reflection. I'm thinking about *La Pasionaria, The* International Brigades and psychedelic tigers as I descend into the Stygian depths of Stereo. Moving between worlds. From light into darkness and a prelude to shortly having all body molecules rearranged by the shamanic noise rituals of Nazoranai: Keiji Haino, Stephen O'Malley and Oren Ambarchi. Sound as alchemy, carried within, back through the city, as, after the show, I head for the train in the warm, dark night.

Haino I

Ambarchi / Haino

Now playing: Stephen O'Malley – *Salt*

13th July 2013

Faust - All Things Must Pass

Delightful and profound cultural 'happenings' at the last *Le Weekend* festival which has taken place at The Tolbooth in Stirling over the past thirteen years. Arguably, the most inventive, adventurous music festival in the UK, it has consistently delivered a stellar mix of old and new sounds, film and 'happenings' which cut across and dissolve styles and genres. On the purely musical front, this year's line-up included highlights such as Ben Frost's glacial noise minimalism, a new commissioned piece *Oceans of Silver and Blood* and Marilyn Crispell's stunning piano improvisations.

One of the most enjoyable events for the collective was an audience with Jean-Herve Peron and Zappi Diemer from the legendary, iconoclastic, Faust. A touch of Fluxus style performance as they riffed on the theme of the festival: *All Things Must Pass*. Diemer, filmed and projected the room/audience in real-time whilst another screen projected some legendary performances of the band. Peron recited some text whilst performing drip painting and gradually uncovering the layers of wrapping over a lumpen shape to reveal their iconic cement mixer. It all worked seamlessly, carried by Peron's infectious enthusiasm and charisma. What was of most interest, however was how the 'setting' had made an impression on his text. He recounted how he had been wandering in the graveyard next to the Church of the Holy Rude, blown away by the spectacular outlook from the ridge under the Castle with its vista onto the landscape of centuries of Scottish history - Stirling Bridge, The Wallace Monument, Highlands to the North, Fife to the East.... All of this had made an impact on Peron and was reflected in this clearly psychogeographically inspired happening.

The other event of the festival that stood out for the collective was a realisation of Alvin Lucier's *I am sitting in a room*. Lucier's electro acoustic music and sound installations have long explored the physical properties of sound itself, the limits of auditory perception and the resonating properties of material objects. In this piece, which by its very nature is unique in every performance, he examines the specific dimensions, acoustic properties and atmospheres of certain rooms.

The realisation took place in The Cowane Hospital, built next door to the The Church of the Holy Rude between 1637 and 1649. John Cowane aka the poetically named 'auld staney breeks' was a very wealthy Stirling merchant and Dean of the Merchant Guild who left funds for this building to be used as an alms house and the maintenance of thirteen elderly Guild members. It was also used for many years as the Guildhall where the Merchants gathered for meetings and dinners. The Guildry fixed the prices of goods, and dominated town council affairs. Later the building was used as a schoolhouse and a hospital during epidemics. It is once again being used for concerts, meetings and ceilidhs, but the statue of John Cowane above the entrance and the portraits of Guild Deans inside remind us of its multi-layered history.

It is said that at midnight on Hogmanay the statue of Cowane will come to life and do a little jig in the forecourt before returning to his post. To return to Lucier's piece, it works by recording a short speech text which is then played back into the room where it is again re-recorded. The new recording is then once again played back and re-recorded, and this process is repeated over and over. Since all rooms have a characteristic resonance, the effect is that certain frequencies are gradually emphasised as they resonate in the room. Eventually the words become unintelligible, replaced by the pure resonant harmonies and tones of the room itself. This process takes around 45 mins in Lucier's recorded version. I forgot to check how long the Cowane Hospital realisation lasted but it did not seem as long as 45 mins although by its very nature, 'time' appears to become suspended as one is drawn in by the minute variations of each repetition. It is a very meditative piece and sitting in the oak panelled room, with the fading light, dribbling through the stained glass windows, all those years of history appeared to be isolated in these ghostly, disembodied harmonies.

Now playing: Faust - *The Faust Tapes*

21st November 2010

Three Gateways

≈

three gateways

a flow   of

spring light

warming stone

~

Hunter Square Edinburgh
15th February, 2014

A Saunter through Summerhall

Buildings loom over us and persist beyond us. They have the perfect memory of materiality

Longevity has no chance without a serious structure

Stewart Brand - *How Buildings Learn*

We finally got the chance to have a good investigative wander around the Summerhall building. Just in time before the Edinburgh Art Festival exhibitions close.

Summerhall is the old Dick Vet building (The Royal (Dick) School of Veterinary Studies of the University of Edinburgh) which has now been transformed into what must be one of the most unique art and performance spaces in the UK. (Europe/World/Cosmos?).

A previous visit was during the full-on party atmosphere of the Edinburgh Festival. Archie Shepp was performing in the Dissection Room, blowing his fire music and détourning jazz standards for the animal spirits. Quite a contrast to a September Saturday when you could wander through the

345

building and its environs and rarely encounter another soul. With over 500 rooms, located over three floors, a basement and outbuildings, wandering the footprint of Summerhall is more like exploring a Borgesian labyrinth where encounters and exhibits are chanced upon and randomly discovered. Quite unlike the mapped-out, directional flow of the conventional gallery experience. Even spending most of the day at Summerhall, we still didn't 'find' everything that was here - around thirty discrete exhibitions that are incorporated into the existing fabric of the building.

And what a building. Whispering from the walls and corridors, you can sense the stories and sounds that are soaked into this space. Stories not only of the human, but also the animals who have inhabited and passed through here: the corridors, the stables, the animal hospital, the dissection rooms...

Above the Entrance to 7x7th Street

First exhibition stop is the playful outdoor installation *7x7* by Jean Pierre Muller in collaboration with seven musicians: Robert Wyatt, Archie Shepp, Sean O'Hagan, Mulatu Astatke, Kassin, Nile Rodgers and Terry Riley. Muller and his stellar band of sonic explorers have created *7x7th Street* consisting of seven wooden huts linked to a letter, a colour of the rainbow, a day of the week, a chakra, and a specific place. Riffing on these associations, each musician has then created an interactive sound sculpture tapping into their own diverse personal histories to create "new connections of knowledge, meaning and poetry".

Robert Wyatt's hut is 'A' for the Alhambra, the Red Palace. Monday, the first day of the week, so the day of the Moon.

Robert Wyatt *7x7*

Inside Wyatt's Alhambra, everything is under the influence of *Clair de Lune.* Audrey Hepburn strums a guitar and sings *Moon River*, Louis Hardin, aka Moondog, keeps watch over the lunar rockets and Neil Armstrong prepares for take-off.

Robert Wyatt *7x7* Interior

Archie Shepp's hut is 'B' for the Blues and the B-line to Brooklyn. The colour of orange sits well with Tuesday, the day of Mars.

347

Archie Shepp 7x7

Archie Shepp *7x7* Interior detail

Perhaps our favourite is **Terry Riley's** 'G' for Galaxies, the colour violet and seventh day of the week, Sunday, day of the Sun. A hut of the Cosmos, the domain of The Sun King,

Terry Riley 7x7

Terry Riley *7x7* Interior detail

What is noticeable in Terry Riley's interior panel is a much reduced number of visual elements. Instead, symbols and motifs are treated to repetition, distortion, diffraction and linked up through connecting space. Much like Riley's music!

A few pictures from the other huts:

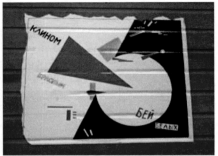

After the jaunty, neo-pop art of *7x7th Street*, a sharper contrast could not be made visiting the Old Stables. Tucked in behind Robert Wyatt's hut, this is the scene of **Robert Kuśmirowski's** installation *Pain Thing*. There is a palpable change in atmosphere as you enter the building from the street. The colours of *7x7 Street* leach out of the retina and fade to dirty cream and grey. Flecks of what looks like dried blood stain the floor and an oppressive air starts to envelop and smother. When we arrive in the main room - an asthmatic room - it feels like we are witnessing the aftermath of some post-apocalyptic scene. An animal experimentation zone where something has gone horribly wrong. The paraphernalia and apparatus of the medical research establishment lies around, test tubes, bell jars, pumps and instruments, some scattered on the floor. The torso of a unidentified creature lies on a hospital style trolley, limbs severed, bone sliced through:

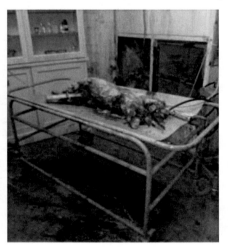

This is not a place we wish to linger.

Inside Summerhall, the building retains its institutional air. Long corridors, unmarked closed doors, stairwells and the cell like structures of the basement. Signage still indicates past functions: The Post-Mortem Room, The Demonstration Room, The Anatomy Lecture Theatre. It is a great place to simply wander around, listening out for whispered narratives layered into stone, wood and glass. The fabric of the building is also used to good effect. The original laboratory benches are used for display purposes and basement cells exude a sinister ambience. One room hosts what looks like some restraining, torture chair and in another a dark sticky ooze spreads on the floor, apparently the residue from some long decomposed water melons.

Chance discovered highlights include stumbling into **Ian Hamilton Finlay's** *Fewer Laws, More Examples* which examines Finlay's response to and fascination with The French Revolution. An ambivalent mash-up of principle and virtue, but also fear and terror. **Robin Gillanders's** *The Philosopher's Garden Redux* portrays ten photographs taken in the Parc Jean-Jacques Rousseau at Emenonville where Rousseau spent the last years of his life. Each photograph represents one of the ten walks of Rousseau's last (uncompleted) book *Les Reveries du Promeneneur Solitaire* (1782).

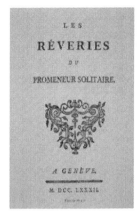

"These hours of solitude and meditation are the only time of the day when I am completely myself"

Jean-Jacques Rousseau

The **Richard Demarco Archives** host a treasure trove of photographs and posters and are a wonderful tribute to Demarco's visionary approach to curating art. There are legendary documented events featuring Joseph Beuys, Marina Abramovich and Tadeusz Kantor and Scottish artists such as George Wyllie and Jimmy Boyle. There is also a reminder that Demarco would take his productions over to Fife with photographs of Valery Anisenko's production of *Macbeth* at Ravenscraig Castle, Kirkcaldy in 1996. A hand scribbled NB reads:

"MacDuff was the Thane of Fife. His Castle lies 8 miles down the Coast" which indeed it still does at East Wemyss. Now a ruin, the site is associated with the MacDuff Earls of Fife, the most powerful family in Fife in the Middle Ages.

Phenotype Genotype (PhG) is a collection of documents, artists books, object multiples catalogues and other ephemera from 1900 to the present day. Displayed on the original college laboratory benches, it is perhaps a bit strange and even disconcerting to see Debord's *La Société du spectacle* and Patti Smith pinbutton badges, displayed like museum exhibits, encased behind glass.

Also in the same room, painted directly on to the wall is *The Periodic Table of Art*. Executed with a certain touch of humour and perhaps also playing upon what appears to be a fundamental human need to catalogue, and document almost anything into a 'meaningful' taxonomy.

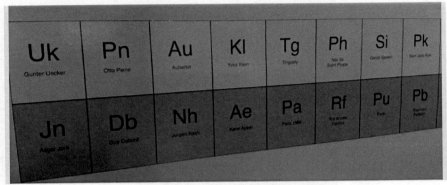

The Periodic Table of Art (Extract)

The absolute standout piece, however, is **David Michalek's** *Figure Studies and Slow Dancing*. An utterly mesmerising, beautiful and thought-provoking 3-screen film installation inspired by the pioneering photography of Eadweard Muybridge. Michalek works with choreographers, dancers, actors and people from the streets of New York and has filmed them, unclothed, performing various 5 second human 'actions' in extreme high-resolution. These 5-second actions are then played back over a period of 7 minutes with every nuance of movement captured on the human body over this elongated time frame. The rich diversity of human form is portrayed across age, gender, ethnic diversity, shape and size. It also raises the question of whether 'class' is written on the unclothed body. This is a work that not only enriches and enthralls but helps you to see the world afresh outside of clock time. The work is further enhanced by the (uncredited) soundtrack which is used to great effect to compliment the images. The unmistakable slow breathing of Morton Feldman's *Piano and String Quartet*.

Just before closing, we are trying to find our way out when we turn a corner and find ourselves facing the iconic image of Joseph Beuys. It is as if he is walking towards us, purposefully, the reflecting light creating a halo around him. As we leave, it is good to know that the spirit of Joseph Beuys is patrolling the corridors of Summerhall. We wonder if the vets ever treated a Coyote?

Beuys Halo - Summerhall

Now Playing: Terry Riley - Descending Moonshine Dervishes

26th September 2012

City Lungs, Breathe at Twilight

City lungs

breathe at twilight

Now playing: AGF - *Breathing in Lines*

17th April 2014

A Huddersfield Bestiary - with Kingfisher

the handsomest by far of all the factory towns in Yorkshire and Lancashire

Friedrich Engels

In hindsight, it was perhaps inevitable. Brought to this town by a Wolf(f) and a Cow, (1) the animistic world was transmitting subtle messages within seconds of walking out of the station.

Directly opposite the grandiose railway building, that could easily masquerade as a town hall, a lion prowls the rooftops, frozen in time since 1853. Those Victorians loved their symbols of Empire and the earthbound relative of our rooftop dweller, gazes out imperiously from the entrance to Lion Chambers. A small winged dragon sits above on the keystone. Possibly a symbol of Victorian industriousness or, as Ruskin would have it, a more sinister, 'satanic' motif of rampant industrialisation. Or perhaps the dragon is simply hiding from St George. I have just walked across a square that bears his name.

I find out later that the present rooftop lion is a fibreglass copy of the original which was made in Coade stone, a ceramic stoneware popular with Victorian and Edwardian architectural sculptors. Other Coade stone lions and decorative statues can be found at Kew Gardens, Buckingham Palace and Westminster Bridge, the present home to London's Red Lion a.k.a The South Bank Lion.

Minutes later I turn a corner to come face to face with the Emporium Dog. All eager eyes and panting tongue. I half expect him to bound up on hind legs to his full height - "Buy Me, Buy Me, Buy Me".

I pass him a few times over the weekend. Always looking happy, as dogs invariably are, when outside in the fresh air. Locked up for the night, he takes on a melancholy countenance, looking out wistfully from his glass cage under the red neon.

I imagine taking him out for the day, navigating on and off trains and buses. A window seat obviously, top deck right at the front. Squeezed into the passenger seat of a car, head out of the window, licking the breeze.

These transmissions from the non-human world became a feature as I wander through Huddersfield over the next few days. I walk up a street named *Beast Market* and regularly see magpies and crows flitting around the small grid of Victorian streets, perfectly at home in their urban environment.

Above what is now a nightclub bar called *Sin*, two fine horses catch the eye. Even with the stone weathering you can see that one is elegant, poised and groomed with a manicured mane.

The other is wild and untamed. Encased in its stone alcove since the 1840s, you can sense its desire to break free and run.

I find out that the building was originally built as a military riding school in the late 1840s and was the headquarters of the 2nd West Yorkshire Yeomanry Cavalry. It subsequently became a music hall in 1905, aptly  named the *Hippodrome* which must have made our wild horse dream of running around the racing stadiums of ancient Greece. Perhaps our groomed stallion was more suited for *hippodrome* chariot racing. I wonder what our horses make of the carnivalesque ambiance of the nightclub bar. Passing outside at night, the dull, techno thud-thud conjuring up the *Taraxippus* - or 'horse disturber' - a ghostly presence blamed for frightening horses at the *hippodromes* throughout ancient Greece. The current 'To Let' sign on the building must create future uncertainty for our equine friends and in a town bristling with the fading lions of Empire, the horses must always remain vigilant.

≈

One thing quickly becomes apparent about Huddersfield. Walk in any direction from the centre of the town and you will soon find that it is completely encased in a ring of traffic.

On a Saturday afternoon and with a bit of time until the next concert, I manage to break through the A62 ring road and head down towards the old industrial mill district, passing the winged lioness and griffins of the Gothic Milton Congregational Church on the way:

I'm drawn to a fairly nondescript, light industrial building. Shuttered and silent it's a colour which has a kind of luminosity, casting light on the road. A premonition of blue?

I'm heading to Bates Mill to see Carlos Casas' audio-visual installation *Avalanche:*

Exploring the interrelation of landscape, soundscape, music and ethnography, Avalanche is an audiovisual meditation about a village and its traditions on the way to disappearance. One of the world's highest inhabited villages, Hichigh is located in Tajikistan's mysterious and fascinating Pamir mountains, home to many archaic and well-kept traditions. The film depicts Hichigh at a time of literal and figurative dusk: on the cusp of becoming a ghost village, just before its stones and mud houses are eaten by the mountain again.

It is a powerful and poignant piece, with the multi-screen environment enhanced by a Phill Niblock score. Depicting a culture barely surviving at subsistence level, they are clinging on to existence on the side of this high mountain landscape and yet, life goes on.

Standing in this space, you cannot help but reflect on the building where this is being exhibited. This old textile mill where the skills, traditions and culture of the yarn spinners was slowly eroded by globalisation, lower cost labour and the flight of international capital. Yet, life goes on. It is good to see Bates Mill now being reinvented as an arts venue, incubator space and photographic studio.

It is late afternoon, drizzly and overcast when I exit Bates Mill. I can hear the River Colne nearby and head off for a quick look. Walking through a deserted car park, a corner of graffiti and greenery, topped off by the pedestrian bridge, punches some colour into the monochrome light. Bizarrely, it looks like the wall has been partly rebuilt, with new bricks erasing part of the original graffiti.

I need to get back to the University where the next event will take place and notice a sign for the Narrow Canal Towpath. How can this be resisted? It feels as if it will take me in the general direction of the University so I enter the narrow opening, casting off the distant traffic sounds with each step as I descend on to the towpath. Looking underneath the arch of the road, which runs overhead, it's no surprise to see the place has been tagged. The water, a still pool of black ink.

I'm heading in the opposite direction. It is so quiet and there is barely any movement on the water as the grey blanket of dusk descends. The phone in my pocket starts to ring and I have barely answered when I'm hit by a jolt of blue at the periphery of vision. Surely not. For I second, I wonder if I've imagined this, when it happens again, like a razor, scything through the twilight which descends to alight barely 10 feet away on the canal bank. A twitching ball of nervous energy, curious. It appears to pull in all the surrounding light and radiate it back. The illuminated blues of lapis lazuli, golden orange, red flecks. A shape-shifting intensity of colours.

"I've just seen a kingfisher, will phone you back"

Of course, it disappeared again as quickly as it had appeared and I was once again left wondering whether I had just imagined this. Up until this day, I had never seen a live kingfisher. I had certainly tried. I had gone to spots along The Water of Leith, in Edinburgh, where there had been sightings and yet they remained elusive. One day I sat on the banks of the Lyne Burn in Fife for hours like a fisherman without a rod, waiting for a glimpse. Anything ... Nothing ... Funny thing is, I doubt if I would have done this for any other bird. I'm not a birder and have little real knowledge of birds, yet they always captivate and fascinate when I stop to look at them. However, the kingfisher has always exerted a strange magic. The name itself - king - fisher - flitting between land and water with a display of colour that shouldn't really belong in this world. As if it this small bird has escaped from a cartoon or wandered in from some exotic climate by accident.

Yet here, today, alongside an old industrial canal I had finally seen one. Of course the bird was long gone but this is where it happened:

Any lingering doubts of having imagined all of this were dispelled when it reappeared one final time. Flying low down the middle of the canal, barely above the water. It almost seemed to be a gesture to confirm its existence. A life enhancing presence in the most unlikely of settings.

Those animistic spirits had clearly been working in my favour.

Now playing: Lyndsay Cooper – *Rags*

11th January 2015

Reference:

Huddersfield Heritage - Leaflet produced by Huddersfield Local History Society, Huddersfield Civic Society and Kirklees Council.

(1) In town for the fantastic Huddersfield Contemporary Music Festival. On this particular weekend two of the major events were concerts featuring Christian Wolff and Henry Cow. Christian Wolff is the last surviving member of the composers who came to be called The New York School alongside John Cage, Morton Feldman and Earle Brown. Wolff is also the person who gave John Cage his first copy of the *I-Ching*. Henry Cow and associated musicians reformed to celebrate the music of composer and multi-instrumentalist Lindsay Cooper (1951 - 2013).

16th January 2015

Acknowledgements

Much thanks to Jerry and Jane Dickens for initiating and helping to bring this project to fruition. A huge thanks to David Gear for allowing his father's paintings to be used in the book and to Lindsay Brown (aka Stray Seal) for the haunting underwater photographs of the Quarry. And the good-natured patience award and great thanks to Rich Elson who managed to construct a ten minute video from a collection of static images and a barely comprehensible Scottish voice-over.

A community of psychogeographers, walkers, artists, poets and generally interesting people have been enormously supportive and encouraging of the activities of the FPC in ways they may not even be aware of. So thank you: Clare Archibald, Aubrey, Matt Barnes, Norrie Bissell and the Geopoeticians, all of the Luther Blissetts, Emma Bolland, Owen Booth, David Borthwick, Peter Boughton, Kenny Brophy, Carringtonia, Matthew Clegg, Alex Cochrane, David Cooper, Jo Dacombe, Paul Dobraszczyk, Cathy Dreyer, DrH Comics, Ian Fenton, Matt Gilbert, Diana J. Hale, Margaret Hannah, Hamer the Framer, Steve Hanson, Ian Hill, Julian Hoffman, Brian Lavelle, Tom Lecky, Brian Lewis, Lines of Landscape, Fraser MacDonald, Gavin MacGregor, Andrew Male, Laurence Mitchell, Marcus O'Dair, Susan Oliver, Andrew Phillips, Eddie Proctor, Andrew Ray, Emina Redzic, Gareth Rees, John Rogers, Jane Samuels, Bobby Seal, The Haunted Shoreline, David Southwell, Katrina Spectrascopic, Calum Storrie, Paul Sullivan, Siân Lacey Taylder, Ben Thompson, Phong Tran, Leigh Wright.

For A, F & R with love.

Music and Soundtracks

About the Music

It is perhaps worth mentioning something about the music references that appear throughout this book and on the original blog.

We know that many psychogeographers and walkers actively incorporate listening to music on headphones as part of their walking practice. However, it is fair to say that in almost all field trips of the FPC, music is **never** listened to whilst actually walking. Certain songs and sounds may involuntarily trip into the mind sparked by some environmental influence but never through an earphone bud.

So what are the 'Now Playing' references?

These started as simply a record of fact, i.e. what was being listened to whilst the piece was being written. Initially, it could be a fairly random collision between music and subject matter. However, as more posts were added, a more conscious approach started to happen with at least some broad connection between music and content. The music then became part of a ritualistic process whenever a new post was published. As the send button was pressed, the 'Now Playing' music would be filling the room to aid the words on their way through the digital ether.

Soundtracks of 2014:

John Luther Adams – *Become Ocean* (Cantaloupe Music).
Oren Ambarchi – *Quixotism* (Editions Mego)
Bohren & Der Club of Gore – *Piano Nights* (PIAS/Ipecac)
Carla Bozulich – *Boy* (Constellation)
Laura Cannell – *Quick Sparrows Over the Black Earth* (Braw)
Dylan Carlson – *Gold* (Oblique)
John Chantler – *Even Clean Hands Damage the Work* (Room 40)
Richard Dawson – *Nothing Important* (Weird World)
Arne Deforce & Mika Vainio – *Hephaestus* (Editions Mego)
Einstürzende Neubauten – *Lament* (Mute)
Kayo Dot – *Coffins on IO* (The Flanser).
Kevin Drumm – *Trouble* (Editions Mego)
Earth – *Primitive And Deadly* (Southern Lord)
Lawrence English – *Wilderness of Mirrors* (Room40)
Morton Feldman - Philip Thomas and John Tilbury *Two Pianos And Other Pieces, 1953-1969* (Another Timbre)
Keith Jarrett/Charlie Haden - *Last Dance* (ECM)
Catherine Lamb – *Matter Moving* (Winds Measure Recordings)
Brian Lavelle – *Prelapsarian* (private physical edition)
S/T – *Lumen Drones* (ECM)
Mogwai – *Rave Tapes* (Rock Action Records)
Gruff Rhys – *American Interior* (Turnstile)
Swans – *To Be Kind* (Young God Records)
United Bible Studies – *Doineann* (A Year in the Country)
Various Artists – *West Coast Soundings* (Edition Wandelweiser Records)
Ian Watson *Caermaen* (Dust, Unsettled)

Most appreciated re-releases:

Cardiacs – *Sing to God* (The Alphabet Business Concern)
John Coltrane – *Offering: Live at Temple University* (Impulse)
Miles Davis - *Miles at the Fillmore* (The Bootleg Series Vol 3 Columbia Legacy)
Jon Hassell – *City: Works of Fiction* (All Saints)
Annette Peacock - *I Belong To A World That's Destroying Itself* (Ironic)
Marshall Allen Presents Sun Ra and his Arkestra – *In the Orbit of Ra* (Strut)

Live Highlights:

Harry Partch's Delusion of the Fury - EIF, Edinburgh
Henry Cow – Lawrence Batley Theatre Huddersfield
Merzbow - 渋谷WWW Tokyo
Mogwai & The Pastels – The Usher Hall Edinburgh
The Pop Group - The Voodoo Rooms Edinburgh
Akio Suzuki – Super Deluxe Tokyo
Swans - The Arches Glasgow
Television – ABC Glasgow
Almost everything at Tectonics and Counterflows festivals in Glasgow and
Huddersfield Contemporary Music Festival.

Soundtracks of 2013

Éliane Radigue, Occam Ocean, at Collège des Bernardins, Paris

A Musical Year: Soundtracks of 2013

Heroine of the year: **Éliane Radigue.**

As Radigue approaches her 82nd birthday, 2013 finally saw a release for Ψ *847*, her
c. 80 min electronic piece originally conceived in 1973. Important Records also
reissued the rare and monumental *Adnos I-III* and just before the year end Shiiin
released the first complete recording of *Naldjorlak I II III*. All of this recorded
documentation was rounded off by being lucky enough to catch a concert in Paris
of her ongoing *Occam Ocean* series of compositions for her trusted acoustic

collaborators: Charles Curtis, Carol Robinson, Bruno Martinez, Robin Hayward, Julia Eckhardt, and Rhodri Davies.

Hero of the year: **Ilan Volkov.**

Curator of the world class *Tectonics* festival in Glasgow and (Reykjavik) bringing together works by composers such as Alvin Lucier, Morton Feldman, Iancu Dimitrescu, Ava-Maria Avram and Hanna Tuulikki. A highlight was watching Alvin Lucier lift the lid off his sonic teapot. Performers included Oren Ambarchi, Stephen O'Malley, Aidan Moffat, Hildur Guðnadóttir and Volkov himself who took part in a rousing version of Ambarchi's *Knots*. In addition, Volkov continues to spearhead 'new' orchestral music and has conducted the BBC SSO in many fine performances including works at The Proms by Cage, Feldman, Varèse and Cardew alongside emerging, contemporary composers.

A big shout out also to the *Counterflows* festival. Another world class event for Glasgow which in 2013 included Loren Connors and Suzanne Langille, Phill Niblock, Jandek, Lina Lapelyte and a blistering closing set from Peter Brötzmann and Paal Nilssen-Love. The line-up for 2014 is already looking pretty fabulous.

So in alphabetical order:

The Dead C - Armed Courage (Ba Da Bing)

What they always do, very well.

Kevin Drumm - *Tannenbaum* (Hospital Productions)

Often reduced to the 'noise' tag. Drumm has produced some incredible deep drone music over the past few years. This is a long, unfolding masterpiece. All 2.5 hours of it.

The Fall - *Re-Mit* and The *Remainderer*

Because anything by The Fall is worthy of celebration.

Fire! Orchestra - *Exit!* (Rune Grammofon)

The big band spirit of Sun Ra lives.

Bruce Gilbert & BAW - *Diluvial* (Touch)

Sounding global warming.

Ramon Humet and The London Sinfonietta - *Niwa* (Neu)

Zen gardens, haikus in sound.

The Incredible String Band - *Live at the Fillmore 1968* (Hux Records)

Long available as a bootleg, but good to have a decent recording which captures the ISB at their creative peak. "They tell me I was there" - Robin Williamson.

Keith Jarrett - *No End* (ECM)

Bit of a lo-fi curio but a fascinating glimpse into the Jarrett mind (or self-indulgent noodling depending on preference). Essentially a home recorded *guitar* album from 1986, but only recently released. (He also plays bass, drums, tablas, percussion, recorder, and piano).

Dennis Johnson - *November* (Irritable Hedgehog)

Tremendous piece of archive reconstruction from Kyle Gann and admirably recorded by Andrew Lee. Jeremy Grimshaw's book on La Monte Young fills in some of the back story on this 'forgotten' work and Johnson's friendship with Young.

Brian Lavelle - *My hands are ten knives* (Quiet World)

BL has built up a fascinating body of sound work, both solo and in collaboration. Very much enjoyed a more minimal direction in 2013 and could easily have chosen *56 Revealings* which was another fine release.

Alan Licht - *Four Years Older* (Editions Mego)

Blue Humans, Text of Light. Noisy guitar poet

Roscoe Mitchell - *Not Yet* (mutable music)

Stunning set of concert compositions. Features conductor Petr Kotik who will be familiar to the Cage/Feldman crowd.

Mogwai - *Les Revenants*

Never caught the TV series but the music stands up very well on its own. A January release for *Rave Tapes* should get 2014 well underway.

Mohammad - *Som Sakrifis* (PAN)

Deep, elemental, drone chamber trio.

The Necks and Evan Parker - Late Junction Session, BBC Radio 3

Open is the first Necks album that I found a bit disappointing. In contrast, this session with Evan Parker was a real treat and much more satisfying. A rare collaboration for The Necks.

Phill Niblock - *Touch Five*

What he always does, very well.

Nohome - *Nohome* (Trost) (Caspar Brötzmann, Marino Pliakas, and Michael Wertmüller)

Lost track of Brötzmann's activity in the past few years, but this is phenomenal. Teaming up with sometime rhythm section of Peter B plus FM Einheit. Melting walls, sonic attack.

Jim O'Rourke - *Steamroom 1 & 5*

These were the only ones we heard of the digital *Steamroom* series and are superb. The rest probably are as well.

The Pastels - *Slow Summits* (Domino)

Welcome album return and the soundtrack to the summer.

Pere Ubu - *The Lady From Shanghai* (Fire Records)

As original and inventive as ever. A holiday in Berlin coincided with a live show. David Thomas luxuriated in overt cantankerousness and necked a bottle of red wine in short order. Table tennis sounds, Ring my Bell

Michael Pisaro - *Tombstones* (Human Ear Music)

Almost a Julia Holter album. Technically 2012 but CD out in 2013.

Éliane Radigue - *Ψ 847* (Oral); *Adnos I-III* (Important); *naldjorlak I II III* (Shiiin).

You have to experience Radigue. Words fail. Meditation helps.

Shampoo Boy - *Licht* (Blackest Ever Black)

Terrible name, but dense, ear pleasing drone from Peter Rehberg & friends.

Splashgirl - *Field Day Rituals* (Hubro)

An even worse name but combine them Shampoo Boy and you could have a Robert Rodríguez film. A piano trio produced by Randall Dunn with some guest appearances from Eyvind Kang.

Burkhard Stangl - *Unfinished. For William Turner, painter* (Touch)

Minimal guitar saturated with atmospheres.

Jakob Ullmann – *fremde zeit addendum 4* (Edition RZ)

Needs full attention.

Water of Life - s/t

Exquisite, art-science collaboration between <u>Rob St.John</u> and <u>Tommy Perman</u> exploring flows of water through Edinburgh using drawings, photos, writing and sound.

Wire - *Change Becomes Us* (Pink Flag)

Still waving the Pink Flag.

Live Highlights:

Acid Mothers Temple - Nice 'n' Sleazy, Glasgow

At their genre shredding best in a small basement club.

Dick Gaughan - Carnegie Hall, Dunfermline

A man with a guitar, a sense of history and political commitment. Great raconteur as well.

Dieter Moebius - Live score to Fritz Lang's *Metropolis* - The Arches, Glasgow

Part of Sonic Cineplex at The Arches Glasgow.

Meredith Monk - *On Behalf of Nature* - Lyceum, Edinburgh

Theatre/music piece inspired by Gary Snyder.

Mogwai, performing live to *Zidane, A 21st Century Portrait* - Broomielaw, Glasgow.

An outdoor, summer gig in Glasgow.

Nazoranai (Keiji Haino, Stephen O'Malley, and Oren Ambarchi) - Stereo Glasgow.

Easily the loudest gig ever witnessed. Earplugs next time but exhilarating

Pere Ubu - Quasimodo, Berlin

See above.

Éliane Radigue, Compositions from *Occam Ocean* - Collège des Bernardins, Paris

This music/sound rearranges the molecules of the body. A big thanks to A who came along on what was a romantic weekend.

Il Sogno del Marinaio (Mike Watt/Stephan Pilia/Andrea Belfi) - Mono, Glasgow.

Mike Watt is always interesting live and intrigued to see Pilia in this setting having previously loved his *Action, Silence Prayers* album.

Patti Smith and Philip Glass, *The Poet Speaks* (A tribute to Allen Ginsberg) - Playhouse, Edinburgh

Was a bit apprehensive about this beforehand, as in may not equal the sum of parts, but what a superb evening. Patti expressed her admiration for Robert Louis Stevenson as well.

Television - The Sage, Gateshead

A rare chance to see a favourite band so well worth a trip to Newcastle and saw Schwitters' Merzbarn wall the next day.

Neil Young & Crazy Horse - SECC, Glasgow

Broke my vow to never visit the SECC again and found electric Neil and the Horse in fine form. Out mbv'd mbv.

Soundtracks of 2012

Selected Soundtracks 2012

Our soundtracks of 2012 have been characterised by works of *substance:*

371

- the long take and the inner journey

    - sounds captured at the threshold of perception

- sounds that affect the body

      - sounds to dwell in

- sounds to travel in.

≈≈≈

Our top 30 in alphabetical order:

Alog - *Unemployed* (Rune Grammofon) (Full 4xLP version)
Oren Ambarchi - *Audience of One* (Touch)
Oren Ambarchi - *Sagittarian Domain* (Editions Mego)
Oren Ambarchi and Thomas Brinkmann - *The Mortimer Trap* (Black Truffle)
John Cage - *John Cage 100 Box* (Wergo)
Don Cherry - *Organic Music Society* (Caprice) (Reissue)
Sidsel Endresen & Stian Westerhus - *Didymoi Dreams* (Rune Grammofon)
Jean-Claude Eloy - *Yo-In* (Hors Territoires)
Erstlaub - *Marconi's Shipwreck* (Broken20)
Morton Feldman – *Crippled Symmetry: At June in Buffalo* (Frozen Reeds)
Fougou - *Further From the Centre of Disturbance* (Greengage Sounds)
Hallock Hill - *The Union | A Hem Of Evening* (MIE)
Thomas Köner – *Novaya Zemlya* (Touch)
Gregg Kowalsky and Jozef Van Wissem - *Movements in Marble and Stone* (Amish)
Brian Lavelle - *The Night Ocean* (Dust, Unsettled)
Locrian and Mamiffer - *Bless Them That Curse You* (Profound Lore)
Bunita Marcus - *Sugarcubes* (TESTKLANG)
Now Wakes the Sea - *Hot Cygnet Tape* (The Geography Trip)
Duane Pitre – *Feel Free* (Important Records)
Porter Ricks - *Biokinetics* (Type) (Reissue)
Eliane Radigue - *Feedback Works 1969-1970* (Alga Marghen)
Akos Rozmann -*12 Stationer VI* (Ideologic Organ)
Richard Skelton – *Verse of Birds* (Corbel Stone Press)
Sleep Research Facility - *Stealth* (Cold Spring)
Wadada Leo Smith – *Ten Freedom Summers* (Cuneiform Records)
Jakob Ullmann – *Fremde Zeit – Addendum* (Edition RZ)
Mika Vainio / Kevin Drumm / Axel Dörner / Lucio Capece - *Venexia* (PAN)
Stian Westerhus - *The Matriarch And The Wrong Kind Of Flowers* (Rune Grammofon)
WITCH - *We Intend to Cause Havoc* (Now Again) (Reissue)
Nate Wooley - *The Almond* (Pogus)

♦♦♦

And a further fiery five of fun:

Elephant9 With Reine Fiske - *Atlantis* (Rune Grammofon)
Goat - *World Music* (Rocket Recordings)

Motorpsycho and Ståle Storløkken - *The Death Defying Unicorn* (Rune Grammofon)
Oren Ambarchi / Fire! - *In the Mouth - A Hand* (Rune Grammofon)
Neil Young with Crazy Horse - *Psychedelic Pill* (Reprise)

Live Highlights:

Afternoon Tea (Ambarchi/Fennesz/Rowe/Rehberg/Pimmon) - HAU2, Berlin
Be a Hobo, The Music of Moondog - Carnegie Hall, Dunfermline
John Cage @ 100 Concert - John Tilbury, RSNO, Ivan Volkov, City Halls, Glasgow
The Fall - The Arches, Glasgow. (On the basis that any Fall gig that is not a complete car crash these days is a highlight)
Morton Feldman, *Coptic Light* and Charles Ives, *The Unanswered Question* - RSNO, David Robertson, Usher Hall, Edinburgh
Morton Feldman, *SQ2* - The Smith Quartet, City Halls, Glasgow
Tim Hecker - Pilrig St Paul's Church, Edinburgh
Archie Shepp - Summerhall, Edinburgh
Patti Smith - ABC, Glasgow
Supersonic Festival - The Custard Factory, Birmingham
Now Playing: Bee Mask - *Vaporware/Scanops*

Soundtracks of 2011:

Aethenor - *En Form For Blå* (VHF)
Alog - *Unemployed* (Rune Grammofon)
Asva - *Presences of Absences* (Important)
Bee Mask - *Elegy for Beach Friday* (Spectrum Spools)
Matt Berry - *Witchazel* (Acid Jazz)
Nels Cline/Tim Berne/Jim Black - *The Veil* (Cryptogramophone)
Seth Cluett - *Objects of Memory* (Line)
Loren Connors - *Red Mars* (Family Vineyard)
Corrupted - *Garten der Unbewusstheit* (Nostalgia Blackrain)
Evangelista - *Animal Tongue* (Constellation)
The Fall - *Ersatz GB* (Cherry Red)
Morton Feldman - *Orchestra* (Mode)
Grouper - *AIA* (Yellowelectric)
Hayvanlar Alemi - *Guarana Superpower* (Sublime Frequencies)
Mary Halvorson/Jessica Pavone - *Departure of Reason* (Thirsty Ear)
Hauschka/Hildur Godnadottir - *Pan Tone* (Sonic Pieces)
Tim Hecker - *Ravedeath 1972* (Kranky)
Julia Holter - *Tragedy* (Leaving Records)
Jenny Hval - *Viscera* (Rune Grammofon)
Stephan Mathieu - *A Static Place* (12K)
Aidan Moffat and Bill Wells - Everything's Getting Older (Chemikal Underground)
Mogwai - *Hardcore Will Never Die But You Will* (Rock Action)
The Necks - *Mindset* (ReR Megacorp)
Phaedra - *The Sea* (Rune Grammofon)
Eliane Radigue - *Transamorem/Transmortem* (Important)
Gruff Rhys - Hotel Shampoo (Turnstile)
Steve Roden - *Proximities* (Electronic)
Sakata/O'Rourke/Chikamorachi - *And That's the Story of Jazz* (Family Vineyard)

Craig Taborn - *Avenging Angel* (ECM)
Anna Thorvaldsdottir - *Rhizoma* (Innova)
Hallock Hill - *The Union* (Hundred Acre)

Most appreciated re-releases:

Alice Coltrane - *Universal Consciousness/Lord of Lords* (Impulse)
Alice Coltrane - *Huntington Ashram Monastery/World Galaxy* (Impulse)
Dinosaur L - *24-24 Music* (Sleeping Bag)
Rolf Julius - *Music for a Distance* (Western Vinyl)
Annette Peacock - *I'm The One*
Eliane Radigue - *Geelriandre/Arthesis* (Senufo)
Franca Saachi - En (Die Schachtel)
Pharoah Sanders - *Village of the Pharoahs/Wisdom Through Music* (Impulse)

Specific Tracks:

Boris - Attention Please
Deerhoof - Behold a Marvel in the Darkness
P.J. Harvey - The Glorious Land
Lana Del Rey - Video Games

Live Highlights:

John Tilbury playing Cage's Sonatas and Interludes, Glasgow
Eliane Radigue Retrospective, London
Jonathan Harvey - Triptych, Edinburgh
Cardew's - The Great Learning (extract) Glasgow
Mogwai - Barrowlands, Glasgow